IRAQ AND SYRIA GENOCIDE EMERGENCY RELIEF AND ACCOUNTABILITY

HEARING

BEFORE THE

SUBCOMMITTEE ON AFRICA, GLOBAL HEALTH, GLOBAL HUMAN RIGHTS, AND INTERNATIONAL ORGANIZATIONS

OF THE

COMMITTEE ON FOREIGN AFFAIRS HOUSE OF REPRESENTATIVES

ONE HUNDRED FIFTEENTH CONGRESS

FIRST SESSION

OCTOBER 3, 2017

Serial No. 115–84

Printed for the use of the Committee on Foreign Affairs

Available via the World Wide Web: http://www.foreignaffairs.house.gov/ or http://www.gpo.gov/fdsys/

U.S. GOVERNMENT PUBLISHING OFFICE

27–060PDF WASHINGTON : 2017

CONTENTS

Page

WITNESSES

The Honorable Frank Wolf, distinguished senior fellow, 21st Century Wilber-
 force Initiative (former U.S. Representative) 5
Shireen, Yazidi survivor of ISIS enslavement 11
Ms. Lauren Ashburn, managing editor and anchor, Eternal Word Television
Network 15
Mr. Stephen Rasche, legal counsel, Director of Internationally Displaced Per-
sons Assistance, Chaldean Catholic Archdiocese of Erbil 19

LETTERS, STATEMENTS, ETC., SUBMITTED FOR THE HEARING

The Honorable Frank Wolf: Prepared statement 8
Shireen: Prepared statement 13
Ms. Lauren Ashburn: Prepared statement 17
Mr. Stephen Rasche: Prepared statement 22

APPENDIX

Hearing notice 42
Hearing minutes 43
Mr. Stephen Rasche:
    Proposal to USAID (Ninevah Reconstruction Committee USA) 44
    Statement of the Heads of the Christian Churches in the Kurdistan Region
    on the Referendum Crisis 52
    Assessing UNDP Minority Projects 55
    U.N. Completed Project for Iraqi Christians 57
    United Nations Development Programme, Funding Facility for Stabiliza-
    tion, Iraq 60
The Honorable Frank Wolf: Northern Iraq 2017 62
The Honorable Christopher H. Smith, a Representative in Congress from
the State of New Jersey, and chairman, Subcommittee on Africa, Global
Health, Global Human Rights, and International Organizations: Written
testimony from Yazda Global Organization 70
Written responses from Mr. Stephen Rasche to questions submitted for the
record by the Honorable Christopher H. Smith 78

IRAQ AND SYRIA GENOCIDE EMERGENCY RELIEF AND ACCOUNTABILITY

TUESDAY, OCTOBER 3, 2017

HOUSE OF REPRESENTATIVES, SUBCOMMITTEE
ON AFRICA, GLOBAL HEALTH,
GLOBAL HUMAN RIGHTS, AND INTERNATIONAL ORGANIZATIONS,
COMMITTEE ON FOREIGN AFFAIRS,
Washington, DC.

The subcommittee met, pursuant to notice, at 12:00 p.m., in room 2172 Rayburn House Office Building, Hon. Christopher H. Smith (chairman of the subcommittee) presiding.

Mr. SMITH. The subcommittee will come to order. And good afternoon to everyone.

In August 2014 ISIS began committing genocide against Christians and Yazidis in Iraq. Three years later those persecuted are still not receiving assistance that they need from the United States, and so their very survival in their ancient homeland is in jeopardy. Two consecutive secretaries of state and the Congress have declared that ISIS is responsible for the genocide.

This year, the President and Vice President declared the genocide and committed the administration to provide relief to the surviving religious and ethnic minority communities. In the final appropriations bill for fiscal year 2017, Congress required that the State Department and U.S. Agency for International Development (USAID) fund the assistance promised by the administration.

Sadly, career staff at the State Department and USAID have ignored the law and thwarted the will of the President, the Congress, and the people we represent. These bureaucrats have refused to direct assistance to religious and ethnic minority communities, even to enable them to survive genocide. This obstruction is unacceptable. And I urge Secretary Tillerson and the new USAID administrator, Mark Green, to put an end to it. I met with Mark a little over a week ago in New York at the U.N. General Assembly, and my hope is that he will act upon that request.

I chaired my first hearing on atrocities against religious and ethnic minorities in Iraq and Syria in September 2013. This hearing today is the tenth I have chaired focusing whole or in part on their plight. Last September I introduced bipartisan legislation, co-authored by my good friend and colleague, Representative Anna Eshoo, explicitly authorizing the State Department and USAID to identify the needs of these communities and fund entities, including faith-based entities, effectively providing them with aid on the ground.

Even though the U.S. has the authority to provide such assistance, we are aware some in the bureaucracy inaccurately claim that they lack the authority, so we wanted to remove this excuse.

It is also important to have a detailed authorization as the foundation for the forthcoming preparations. Partially informed by my own trip to Erbil last December to meet firsthand with genocide survivors, we introduced this legislation again as H.R. 390, almost immediately after the start of the new Congress, with even stronger support from both sides of the aisle, and many Christian and Yazidi accountability human rights groups, and numerous leaders.

The House passed it unanimously in early June. And the Senate Foreign Relations Committee passed it unanimously on September 19th. There has been no subsequent action in the Senate, however. And so I respectfully ask the Senate to immediately pass H.R. 390.

This hearing will explore the urgent crisis for Christians and Yazidi genocide survivors, especially in Iraq; what the administration can do now to enable them to survive; and what the consequences will be for these communities and our national security if we fail to act.

As you will hear from several of our distinguished witnesses, helping these communities survive and return to their homes will reduce threats from Iran. It will also deny ISIS a major propaganda victory and recruiting tool.

Before proceeding to the witnesses I would note that the State Department and USAID were invited to testify at today's hearing. They were unavailable. We will try again and convene yet another hearing in order to try to hear from them.

Our first witness today is known to many of you, perhaps to all of you, my dear friend for many years, the former representative from the 10th District of Virginia, Frank Wolf. He was elected the same year Ronald Reagan got elected in 1981. He is here today as the distinguished senior fellow at the 21st Century Wilberforce Initiative. And he visited northern Iraq again this past August.

In his statement he points out that he believes that if bold action is not taken by the end of the year, he believes a tipping point will be reached, and we will see the end of Christianity in Iraq. Imagine that—the end of Christianity in Iraq. Regarding the Yazidis, although Sinjar has been liberated from ISIS since the fall of 2015, it is currently controlled by multiple different militia groups. Few families have been able to return, and few aid groups work in the area.

Congressman Wolf also raises the alarm about the Iran-backed militias filling the post-ISIS liberation vacuum as part of Tehran's "goal of creating a land bridge from Iran to allow Iran to move fighters, weapons, and supplies to aid Hezbollah and other terrorist groups." He also offers several concrete policy recommendations that the administration and the Congress should heed immediately.

I would note parenthetically that Frank Wolf is a champion on a whole lot of issues but perhaps none more than in the area of international religious freedom. He is the prime author of the 1998 International Religious Freedom Act, landmark legislation that in a multiple of areas established the State Department's Office on Religious Freedom and, most importantly, made it a priority within the administration, including the importance of training Foreign Service officers about religious freedom, about religious institutions, which they had not gotten previously.

It also established the independent Commission on International Religious Freedom which acts as a watch dog, provides its own extraordinarily useful insight as to what needed to be done in the area of religious freedom. And those two major components, the State Department and the independent Commission, have made an enormous difference, and just last Congress passed legislation, named in Frank Wolf's honor, the Frank Wolf International Religious Freedom Act, which took many of the ideas that were gleaned and learned over the course since 1998, put them into law, including the importance of holding individuals who commit acts, crimes, and atrocities against believers to account, and also to create lists of those prisoners of conscience in order to act on their behalf, which is exactly what I know Mr. Wolf had envisioned in his earlier law.

Our second witness will be Shireen, a Yazidi survivor of ISIS enslavement. She wrote in her statement that captivity under ISIS was "like Hell. They performed . . . abdominal surgery on me" and "I am suffering from the effects of it." "They committed all kinds of" atrocities "against us, including mass killing, sexual enslavement, and forced conversion."

Shireen also wrote, and I quote, "19 members of my family and my relatives are missing. They may be killed or still in captivity but we don't know anything about them. We are still waiting for action and the liberation of thousands of Yazidis from ISIS captivity."

She warns that "Yazidis, Christians and other religious minorities, especially the non-Muslim minorities, cannot survive in Syria and Iraq under the current conditions. Without serious action from you," meaning us, the Congress, and the White House, "and the world governments many of these people will continue to flee their ancient homelands of Syria and Iraq."

Our third witness will be Lauren Ashburn, the managing editor and anchor of EWTN News Nightly. She traveled to northern Iraq earlier this year and has continued to report on the crisis. Her story telling and video, rooted in more than 20 years as journalist, has helped to tell the amazing stories of heroism, indomitable faith, and survival for those who have been victimized.

As she reported in her written testimony for this hearing, Christians in Iraq are on the brink of extinction. "The United States is the only nation in the world that can provide concrete aid to rebuild the community that I saw in shambles."

Our fourth and final witness today will be Stephen Rasche, legal counsel and director of the IDP Resettlement Program for the Chaldean Catholic Archdiocese of Erbil, and legal counsel and chief coordinator for the Nineveh Reconstruction Committee.

Mr. Rasche testified before a hearing I chaired on the Helsinki Commission last September. And he had dire news for us then. He reports in his written testimony today, "I regret to say that we still have not received any form of meaningful aid from the United States Government. While we have found the political appointees much more willing to help us since January, the fact is that even after the better part of a year, they have been unable to move the bureaucracy to take meaningful action."

The Obama administration channeled all U.S. funding for stabilization in Iraq through the funding facilities for stabilization administered by the U.N. Development Program, the UNDP. And the current administration, sadly, has continued that policy. Mr. Rasche testified in his written statement, "While status reports of UNDP work in Nineveh purport to show real progress, in the Christian minority towns on the ground we see little evidence of it. Work projects are in most cases cosmetic in nature and much of that cynically so. In effect, U.S. taxpayers are financing the spoils of genocide."

As an alternative option for U.S. assistance he details Nineveh Sustainable Return Program, an initiative of the Ecumenical Nineveh Reconstruction Committee, to repair homes damaged or destroyed by ISIS. The program has already rebuilt several thousand homes and enabled thousands of Christian families to return, mostly funded by the Knights of Columbus and Aid to the Church in Need, with some additional funding from the Government of Hungary.

Last month the Nineveh Reconstruction Committee USA submitted a proposal to USAID to ensure that the project can be completed and many more families can return.

I strongly support this time-sensitive proposal and call on USAID Administrator Green to ensure that a decision is made as soon as possible. Because of the resistance among career staff at USAID to direct the assistance to religious and ethnic minority communities even though they were targeted for genocide, it is imperative that officials appointed by the President are part of the review process, and that the final decision be made by the Presidential appointees.

I am including the proposal as part of the record.

Finally, he says in his testimony, "Today, as I speak to you, we are caught fully exposed and at-risk, finding ourselves at a critical historical inflection point," Congressman Wolf called it a tipping point, "foreign aid decisions over which will determine whether Christianity, and religious pluralism, vital to the U.S. national interest and regional security, will survive in Iraq at all."

Mr. Suozzi, I would like to recognize my good friend for any comments you might have.

Mr. SUOZZI. Mr. Chairman, I just want to thank you for calling attention to this very important issue. Genocide is a real reality of today's world, and ISIS is committing these atrocities. And we need to call attention to what they are doing to these ethnic minorities throughout this entire region.

So I thank you so much for calling attention to this issue. And I look forward to hearing the witness' testimony.

Mr. SMITH. I thank my good friend from New York.

And I would like now to invite our distinguished witnesses to the witness table and so we can begin.

I would like to now welcome Congressman Frank Wolf to present his testimony. Again we thank him for his decades-long commitment to religious freedom. As I said in my comments a moment ago, he is the William Wilberforce of Congress who has made the difference, the difference in religious freedom around the world. His legislation has had consequences that are awe inspiring.

I yield to you.

STATEMENT OF THE HONORABLE FRANK WOLF, DISTINGUISHED SENIOR FELLOW, 21ST CENTURY WILBERFORCE INITIATIVE (FORMER U.S. REPRESENTATIVE)

Mr. WOLF. Well, thank you, Mr. Chairman. I want to thank you for your efforts. And I also want to thank your staff. Your staff has done an outstanding job and I want to thank them and all the members of this subcommittee for this effort.

After a week visiting Bartella, Qaraqosh, Duhok, Erbil, Mosul, Nimrud, Mt. Sinjar, and Sinjar City in August and talking with individuals in the various communities, I am sad to say that if bold action is not taken by the end of the year, I believe a tipping point will be reached and we will see the end of Christianity in Iraq in a few short years and a loss of religious and ethnic diversity throughout the region, a loss which will not be regained and could result in further destabilization and violent extremism and terrorism across the Middle East. In other word, ISIS will have been victorious in their genocidal rampage unless concrete action is taken.

Iraq is a land rich with Biblical history. Abraham was born there, Daniel lived and died there, and many events in the Bible took place in Iraq. And yet, we have already seen the Christian population drop from 1.5 million to 250,000, or less, over the course of the last 14 years. This exodus continues with additional families leaving every day in search of physical security, economic security, and education.

Having spent the past 3 years as Internally Displaced People, IDPs, many Christian families are at a crossroads, having to decide whether or not they should return to their newly liberated villages or leave Iraq forever. Despite their best efforts, many believe that they can stay only if bold action is taken by the United States Government and other international partners to ensure, ensure their future security.

While I was expecting to hear further reports about security concerns related to ISIS, I was surprised to find that most individuals everywhere we went I spoke with were concerned about the various military factions controlling their towns and villages, in particular Hashd al-Shaabi, also known as the Popular Mobilization Force, or PMF. The Hashd al-Shaabi militia, which is backed to a large degree by Iran, and other militia groups are filling the vacuum left post-liberation. This is part of the Iranian goal of creating a land bridge from Iran through Iraq to Syria to reach a port on the Mediterranean. Such a land bridge will allow Iran to move fighters, weapons, and supplies to aid Hezbollah and other terrorist groups. This will be a direct threat to Israel and a direct threat to the United States military, as well as others in the West.

Among the Yazidi community we heard many of the same concerns. Sinjar is a prime example of the complications the minority communities on the ground continue to face. Considered a contested territory by the Central Government and the Kurdistan Regional Government, Sinjar has been liberated from ISIS since the fall of 2015. However, it is currently controlled by multiple different multiple militia groups. Due to this, few families have been able to return.

As we drove through, periodically we would see a little house, but very, very few.

And few aid groups work in the area due to the potentially volatile situation. After having been the victims of genocide, and with 3,000, almost 3,000 of their woman and girls still being held in captivity, one of the Yazidi religious leaders we met with stated, "We just want to be able to live."

Unfortunately, to a large extent, U.S. Government assistance has not been forthcoming to Iraq's Christians and Yazidi communities even though the President, the Vice President, Congress, and Secretary of State have declared them victims of genocide. Many of the displaced Christians, for example, have had to seek the mainstay of their aid from private charitable sources on a piecemeal basis over the last 3 years. This is becoming more difficult, Mr. Chairman, as many individuals who give to humanitarian organizations are facing donor fatigue.

It is imperative that the United States help the Christians and the Yazidis to return to their hometowns. As a U.N. official aptly stated in a recent meeting, they said, "the religious minorities need unique solutions. What works to return Sunni Muslims to Mosul will not work to return religious minorities to contested territories."

Since 2014, Congress has had well over 40 different hearings related to ISIS, including at least seven specifically on the topic of the religious minorities, and required the State Department, the U.S. Agency for International Development to spend some funds on assistance specifically for genocide survivors from religious and ethnic minorities. Congressional resolve, and the force of law, must be matched by administration action.

In closing, some recommendations: 1) Now that the military battle with ISIS is largely over, our Government needs fresh eyes on the target, fresh eyes in Iraq with regard to our current policies, not only for the victims of genocide, and war crimes, and crimes against humanity, but also because of the critical national security interests in the region. Failure to act soon may result in chaos and violence in the region yet again.

The United States has a vested interest in promoting peace and stability in a region where over 4,000 Americans gave their lives and $2 trillion of taxpayer money was spent over the last 13 years. A high-level group of individuals with expertise in the region should be brought together by the administration to do an assessment of the current situation and make recommendations for our policy going forward.

2) A Presidential Decision Directive or Presidential memorandum should be issued directing the State Department and USAID to immediately, to immediately address the needs to communities identified by Secretary Tillerson as having been targeted for genocide. This would address both humanitarian aid for those living as IDPs and refugees, and stabilization assistance for those returning to the areas.

3) A post should be established, it must be established by the White House for an interagency coordinator to guarantee that the

needs of these communities are adequately addressed to ensure their safety and preservation consistent with United States foreign policy. When President Bush appointed Senator John Danforth to be the envoy to work on similar issues in Sudan, the announcement was made in the White House Rose Garden with Senator Danforth standing between President Bush and Secretary of State Colin Powell. This, Mr. Chairman, sent a powerful message to the world, and also to government employees, the suffering people of Sudan also.

And so I recommend the same level of announcement for the person who will fill this position. Keep in mind, personnel is policy. You put the right person and they can get this job done. It should be held at the White House with President Trump and Secretary Tillerson. This will send a message that America is engaged. The Christians and the Yazidis have faced genocide; for the longest period of time the United States and the West has offered little more than words.

Lastly, fourthly, Congress should immediately pass H.R. 390, the bipartisan Iraq and Syria Genocide Emergency Relief and Accountability Act, authored by you and co-authored by Congresswoman Anna Eshoo. It gives explicit authorization for the State Department and USAID to identify the assistance needs of genocide survivors from religious and ethnic minority communities and provide funding to entities, including faith-based entities, effectively providing them with aid on the ground.

It is essential because some within the State Department and USAID have claimed they lack the authority to deliberately help religious and ethnic communities, even if they are genocide victims. They are genocide victims. They may be Christians, they may be Yazidis. They are genocide victims and they will become extinct, extinct without assistance.

Although there is nothing in U.S. law preventing them from helping genocide-surviving communities, the authorization will help ensure that aid actually flows to the victims. The House passed the bill, Senate Foreign Relations passed it on September 19th. The Senate should pass it quickly so it can be sent back to the House and for the President to sign it.

Mr. Chairman, in closing, there is still time but the hour is late. And we are about to run out of time. We cannot—history will judge the administration, the Congress, and the West—allow ISIS to be successful in their genocide.

[The prepared statement of Mr. Wolf follows:]

SUBCOMMITTEE ON AFRICA, GLOBAL HEALTH, GLOBAL HUMAN RIGHTS, &
INTERNATIONAL ORGANIZATIONS
"Iraq and Syria Genocide Emergency Relief & Accountability"
Written Testimony of Cong. Frank R. Wolf (Ret. 1981-2014)
Distinguished Senior Fellow, 21st Century Wilberforce Initiative
October 3, 2017

To begin I would like to thank Chairman Smith and the Members of the Subcommittee for holding this hearing today.

After a week visiting Bartella, Qaraqosh, Duhok, Erbil, Mosul, Nimrud, Mt. Sinjar, and Sinjar City in August and talking with individuals from the various communities, I am sad to say that if bold action is not taken by the end of the year, I believe a tipping point will be reached and we will see the end of Christianity in Iraq in a few short years and a loss of religious and ethnic diversity throughout the region- a loss which will not be regained and could result in further destabilization, violent extremism and terrorism across the Middle East. In other words, ISIS will have been victorious in their genocidal rampage unless concrete action is taken.

Iraq is a land rich with Biblical history. Abraham was born there, Daniel lived and died there and many events of the Bible took place in Iraq. And yet, we have already seen the Christian population drop from 1.5 million to 250,000, or less, over the course of the past 14 years. This exodus continues with additional families leaving every day in search of physical security, economic security and education. Having spent the past three years as Internally Displaced People (IDP's), many Christian families are at a crossroads, having to decide whether or not they should return to their newly liberated villages or leave Iraq forever. Despite their best efforts, many believe that they can stay only if bold action is taken by the US and other international partners to ensure their future security.

While I went expecting to hear further reports about security concerns related to ISIS, I was surprised to find that most individuals I spoke with were concerned about the various military factions controlling their towns and villages- in particular the Hashd al-Shaabi (also known as the Popular Mobilization Forces or PMF). The Hashd-al Shaabi militia, which is backed by Iran, and other militia groups are filling the vacuum left post-liberation. This is part of the Iranian goal of creating a land-bridge from Iran, through Iraq to Syria to reach a port on the Mediterranean. Such a land-bridge will allow Iran to move fighters, weapons and supplies to aid Hezbollah and other terrorist groups. This will be a direct threat to Israel and the United States military as well as others in the West.

Among the Yazidi community we heard many of the same concerns. Sinjar is a prime example of the complications the minority communities on the ground continue to face. Considered a contested territory by the Central Government and the Kurdistan Regional Government, Sinjar has been liberated from ISIS since the fall of 2015, however, it is currently controlled by multiple different militia groups. Due to this, few families have been able to return and few aid groups work in the area due to the potentially volatile situation. After having been the victims of genocide and with 3,000 of their women and girls still in captivity, one of the Yazidi religious leaders we met with stated, "We just want to be able to live."

Unfortunately, to a large extent, U.S. Government assistance has not been forthcoming to Iraq's Christian and Yezidi communities even though the President, Vice President, Congress and Secretary of State have declared them victims of genocide. Many of the displaced Christians, for example, have had to seek the mainstay of their aid from private charitable sources on a piecemeal basis for over three years. This is becoming increasingly difficult as many individuals who give to humanitarian organizations are facing donor-fatigue.

It is imperative that the United States help the Christians and Yazidis to return to their home towns. As a UN official aptly stated in a recent meeting, "the religious minorities need unique solutions." What works to return Sunni Muslims to Mosul will not work to return religious minorities to contested territories.

Since 2014, Congress has had well over 40 different hearings related to ISIS, including at least 7 specifically on the topic of the religious minorities and required the State Department and U.S. Agency for International Development to spend some funds on assistance specifically for genocide survivors from religious and ethnic minorities. Congressional resolve, and the force of law, must be matched by Administration action.

In closing I would like to provide a few recommendations:

1) Now that the military battle with ISIS is largely over, our government needs "fresh eyes" in Iraq with regard to our current policies, not only for the victims of genocide, war crimes and crimes against humanity, but also because of the critical national security interests in the region. Failure to act soon may result in chaos and violence in the region yet again. The United States has a vested interest in promoting peace and stability in a region where over 4,000 Americans gave their lives and $2 trillion dollars of taxpayer money was spent in the past 13 years. A high-level group of individuals with expertise in the region should be brought together to do an assessment of the current situation and make recommendations for our policy going forward.

2) A Presidential Decision Directive or Presidential Memorandum should be issued directing the State Department and USAID to immediately address the needs to communities identified by Secretary Tillerson as having been targeted for genocide. This would address both humanitarian aid for those living as IDP's and refugees and stabilization assistance for those returning to the areas seized from them by ISIS.

3) A post should be established by the White House for an inter-agency coordinator to guarantee that the needs of these communities are adequately addressed to ensure their safety and preservation consistent with United States foreign policy. When President Bush appointed Senator John Danforth to be the Envoy to work on similar issues in Sudan, the announcement was made in the White House Rose Garden with Sen. Danforth standing between President Bush and Secretary of State Colin Powell. This sent a powerful message to the world and the suffering people of Sudan. I recommend the same level of announcement for the person who will fill this position. It should be held at the White House with President Trump and Secretary Tillerson. This will send a message that America is engaged. The Christians and Yazidis have faced genocide and for the longest time the United States and the West has offered little more than words.

4) Congress should immediately pass H.R. 390, the bipartisan Iraq and Syria Genocide Emergency Relief and Accountability Act, authored by Chairman Chris Smith and coauthored by Congresswoman Anna Eshoo. It gives explicit authorization for the State Department and USAID to identify the assistance needs of genocide survivors from religious and ethnic minority communities and provide funding to entities – including faith-based entities – effectively providing them with aid on-the-ground. This is essential, because some within the State Department and USAID have claimed they lack the authority to deliberately help religious and ethnic communities, even if they are genocide victims and will become extinct without assistance. Although there is nothing in U.S. law preventing them from helping genocide-surviving communities, the authorization will help ensure the aid actually flows to the victims. The House passed H.R. 390 on June 6 and Senate Foreign Relations Committee passed it on September 19. The Senate should pass the bill quickly so it can be sent back to the House and then the President for signing.

There is still time, but the hour is late and we are about to run out of time. We cannot allow ISIS to be successful in their genocide.

Mr. SMITH. Thank you very much, Congressman Wolf.
Shireen.

STATEMENT OF SHIREEN, YAZIDI SURVIVOR OF ISIS ENSLAVEMENT

[The following statement and answers were delivered through an interpreter.]

Ms. SHIREEN. My name is Shireen Jerdo Ibrahim. I am a Yazidi girl, a survivor of ISIS from Rambusi village, which is a village on the south side of Mt. Sinjar near Sinjar town.

On August 3rd when we were at home my uncle called me from another village, a Yazidi village, and said that the Peshmerga forces have withdrawn and ISIS attacked our areas. He advised me to leave to the mountain.

We got a few things ready, locked the doors, and got in our trucks and headed toward the mountain. Before we got there our truck broke down, so we decided to continue on foot. At the foothill of the mountain ISIS came with their trucks and captured all of us.

When they stopped us they returned us to a wedding hall which was near Sinjar town. When they unloaded everybody from trucks, right in the front of everyone they executed a young Yazidi man because he wanted to stay with his family.

Then they took us to another building and they separated families. They separated women and men. They separated my younger sister from me. And her hand was in my hand; they separated her from me. And they hit me with a weapon.

They took us to Badoosh which there was a prison in Badoosh that they put all the families with me in there.

Then I was moved from Badoosh Prison to Kashumahar village which is near Tal Afar. And then they sold me to someone in Raqqa in Syria. In Syria I was tortured.

Then I was brought to Mosul. I was told five times when I was in captivity during this time in captivity I was not the only one. I saw many Yazidi girls. There were hundreds and thousands of Yazidi girls there being sold as sex slaves.

I was lucky to be able to escape. But others remained in captivity. Still we have thousands of Yazidi women and boys in captivity. As I speak to you today I have 19 members of my family missing. I have no idea where they are, if they are killed, if they are missing, if they are in captivity.

Our hope was that somebody would help those in captivity and give us a conclusion about what happened to our family members. It's been 3 years. Our hope is that our areas were going to be rebuilt, some security will be provided for us after what happened to us. And they will help us, you know, free those in captivity, our family members.

It is true that the United States and the many other countries recognize what happened to Yazidis as a genocide. But our hope was that this would be followed by action: Our areas will be rebuilt and security will be provided. They will take those who committed crimes against us and who sold us as sex slaves will be brought to justice, and not let them get away with what they did. Our hope is that Yazidis will be assured that they will be able to go back to their homes, or if they can't live in their homes they will be able to immigrate somewhere else because it is not easy for them to go back again and live under the same conditions.

You know, when ISIS came their goal was to eradicate Yazidis and Christians from Iraq. Their main goal was to attack them. And they succeeded. They displaced all of us. They murdered many Yazidis. And Yazidis and Christians and other small minorities will not be able to live there under the same environment.

I mean it is out there, what ISIS did to us is out there. It is known to everyone. They displaced thousands. They killed thousands of Yazidis. Inside the liberated areas we see mass graves, almost every week we see mass graves. There are about 40 mass graves so far. Some people see bones for their relatives, but others don't even know if their relatives were executed or still in captivity.

There are hundreds, if not thousands, of boys who were rescued or escaped from ISIS captivity living in camps, in IDP camps. Some of them don't even speak their own language, they speak Arabic because of what ISIS did to them.

Those families who lost members, many members, just like my family, they have been living in these IDP camps for 3 years under the same tents. Families don't have income. They don't have a way of living in these camps. So it has been 3 years and people are looking for a solution.

Our hope is that whoever can hear me today, or all of you, can help those Yazidis who are rescued. If they are rescued that doesn't necessarily mean they are okay. Some of them living in camps are traumatized. They need psychological and social support. They need a home to live in, not a camp that had been set up 3 years ago.

So, our hope is that a real solution will be provided for those families who suffered under ISIS.

We heard reports that some Yazidi boys even ended up in Saudi Arabia. They sold them to each other. They brainwashed them. They trained them. We don't know anything. Almost all of Iraq is liberated now and thousands are missing; we don't know what happened to them. Families are looking for their members. They have no idea what to do.

We are hoping that something will be done, and quickly done. It has been 3 years and the solution is not there yet. We haven't seen any action in this regard.

It is true that ISIS has been pushed out from Iraq but the ideology remains there. So even if they are gone, as Yazidis and Christians go back to their homes and there is the same ideology, a different group may attack us. So people are not able to go back unless some security is provided for them and some guarantees.

Thank you for giving me the opportunity to tell my story and the story of my community and the Christian community and what we are suffering in Iraq.

[The prepared statement of Ms. Shireen follows:]

Shireen Jerdo Ibrahim's Testimony

Ladies and gentlemen, Members of Congress, thank you for inviting me.

My name is Shireen Jerdo Ibrahim and I am 31 years old. I am one of the thousands of Yazidi survivors. I grew up in Rambusi village, close to Sinjar town, South side of Mount Sinjar. Prior to August 2014, I was living a simple life with my family in our rural area, however, ISIS came and took over our homeland after the withdrawal of Kurdish Peshmerga forces.

On August 3rd 2014, my sister with her children were visiting us and we were preparing to celebrate our mid-summer feast (festival), when I heard the sound of gun-shots from Gerzarek, Seba Sheikh Khider and Tel-Azer (Yazidi complexes, Southern Sinjar), I called my cousin and my uncle, they said that Peshmerga security forces withdrew from the area and that ISIS has attacked our towns. My relatives advised us to escape.

We prepared some stuff and locked the doors of our house. Then we all got into our little pick-up truck and headed toward Sinjar Mountain. By the time we arrived at the foothills of the Mountain, our vehicle broke down, we decided to continue on foot. While we were walking along the road, three cars loaded with ISIS militants arrived and stopped us, they asked all of us to give up weapons and cell phones. I turned off my phone immediately and putted it inside my sock. My family and I among many other Yazidi families were arrested by ISIS and moved to a wedding hall near Sinjar city.

We were ordered and threatened by ISIS militants to get off the trucks they had loaded us into. After we stepped out of the trucks, the militants shot three bullets into a young Yazidi man's head killing him because he said he wanted to wait for his family to arrive. Our tragedy began from here as they moved all the abducts to the government office inside Sinjar district. ISIS militants separated Yazidi girls for the rest of us by force. My sister, Sahera, was about 15 years old and she was the second girl that was taken. Her hand was in my hand and she was throwing up and crying. She was wearing a dress I had made for her, I was crying and begging them to not take her. One of the militants hit my back with his weapon. Then they forced us all into buses and took us to Badoosh jail.

The jail smelled dirty and there was blood everywhere on the floor. While were all crammed together and terrified, the jail was targeted by US coalition airstrike. As a result, they moved us to Tal-Afar district where ISIS leaders who are responsible for our kidnapping and selling were there. One of them called Haji Mahdi who is from Tel afar and another called Abu Ali from Mosul. I recognized Abu Ali on television when he was escaping from Talafar among IDPs where he was interviewed on Kurdish TV (Rudaw). He is responsible for separating me from my family and selling and enslaving me with many other Yazidi girls. I heard that he now lives in IDPs camp close to Mosul and there is no one to punish him for his crimes against me and against Yazidi community. There are thousands of ISIS militants like Abu Ali who committed crimes against Yazidis and today, they are free without punishment.

From Tel -afar I was sold to a person from Raqa city in Syria, In Raqa they tortured me because I refused to talk. From Raqa they sold me again to a person from Mosul city. I was sold and bought as a cheap commodity for more than five times. Some girls were sold as cheap as few dollars. I spend nine months in captivity under ISIS; it was like hell. They performed an abdominal surgery on me while in Mosul city and until now, I am suffering from the effects of it. I don't know why they operated on me or what kind of a procedure was done on my body. They committed all kinds of atrocious crimes against us including mass killing, sexual enslavement, and forced conversion.

Today as I speak here before you, 19 members of my family and my relatives are missing. They may be killed or still in captivity but we don't know anything about them. Many countries including United states and the United Nations recognized the Yazidi genocide, however our hope was there will be steps following that to provide justice and protection for my people. We are still waiting for action and the liberation of thousands of Yazidis from ISIS captivity. Today, in the liberated areas of Yazidi homeland, there are more than 40 mass graves.

Our homes and lives were destroyed by ISIS, however, we still hope that our homeland will be re-built, so that Yazidis, Christians and other minorities can find peace again, because this was our ancient homeland where we once co-existed as brothers and sisters.

In conclusion, I want to let you know of one thing which I hope you will take serious measures to consider; Yazidis, Christians and other religious minorities, especially the non-Muslim minorities, cannot survive in Syria and Iraq under the current conditions. Without serious action from you and the world governments many of these people will continue to flee their ancient homelands of Syria and Iraq. The protection of these minorities means that one day, my people will not become extinct.

Thank you

Mr. SMITH. Shireen, thank you very much for your very powerful and heartbreaking testimony. It just brings again before the Congress what victims have suffered and continue to suffer. And thank you for your bravery in bringing this forward to us.

Know that all of our prayers are with you. And thank you.

Ms. Ashburn.

Mr. SUOZZI. I just want to add, we want you to know, Ms. Shireen, how courageous it is of you to show up like this. And we are very grateful to you for educating us about what is happening to your family and to other people that you know in your community.

Thank you so much.

STATEMENT OF MS. LAUREN ASHBURN, MANAGING EDITOR AND ANCHOR, ETERNAL WORD TELEVISION NETWORK

Ms. ASHBURN. Chairman Smith, members of the subcommittee, good afternoon. Thank you for inviting me to appear before you today.

In April of this year, I set out with a team from my network, EWTN, including journalists Susanna Pinto, Paul Fifield, and Tom Haller, to report on the plight of Christians and other religious minorities in the northen Iraqi city of Erbil and the Nineveh Plain to the north and east of Mosul. We knew that these groups had suffered genocide, as the U.S. State Department had recognized in March 2016, and we had read their harrowing experiences. But we were not prepared for the death and destruction we were about to witness.

Christians in Iraq are on the brink of extinction. And I saw that grim reality first hand.

My visit to the town of Batnaya in northern Iraq embodies the experience of Christians in that region. Islamic State forces controlled the Christian enclave for 2 years before Kurdish fighters pushed them out in November 2016. As I toured the devastated town, I could hear explosions from the fighting in Mosul, 15 miles away.

What I saw was absolute evil in the form of devastation and destruction. ISIS had flattened 90 percent of Batnaya. The village looked like an earthquake had struck. And the danger is not over. There are signs everywhere there warning of IEDs and booby traps.

The Catholic Church in the center of the town is still standing, only because ISIS used it as a command center. But it has been severely damaged and desecrated. A statue of the Virgin Mary is decapitated. Other statues are smashed to bits. The face of Jesus had been ripped off from paintings. Bullet holes mark the place where a cross once hung. Every Christian symbol I could see had been defaced or obliterated. I could not hold back my tears.

In a nearby graveyard, Christian headstones were uprooted. Even the final resting place was not safe from the fury of the Islamic State.

I spoke with a Christian grandmother and her daughter, who had fled the jihadist onslaught with their family. They sobbed while looking at the damage done to their home. Their whole life was there. They want desperately to return, but they have no money to rebuild, and no money is coming. Still the daughter's husband climbed to the roof and tied a makeshift cross to a metal rod sticking out of it.

Similar scenes can be seen in other Christian towns in the area, including Qaraqosh, which was freed from ISIS in October 2016; it suffered appalling damage. Many Christians in northern Iraq feel abandoned in the aftermath of the U.S.-led war that toppled Saddam Hussein. During my visit, headlines in the U.S. focused on the gas attack in neighboring Syria and two horrifying church bombings in Egypt, which killed dozens and were claimed by the Islamic State. But events in Iraq seldom get as much attention. The American public seems to have moved on.

Despite having survived genocide, Christians and others in northern Iraq want to go back to their homeland.

In Batnaya on Palm Sunday I witnessed a crowd of Christians return for the day for Mass and a procession. At the church, a priest, aided by volunteers, had just spent weeks cleaning up. He conducted the service in Aramaic, the language of Jesus Christ. The altar behind him was covered in rubble. The congregation erected a huge metal cross where the altar used to be, decorated with burning votive candles. They had placed palm branches on the crosses defaced by the Islamic State, a small symbol of hope over hate.

The United States is the only nation in the world that can provide concrete aid to rebuild this community that I saw in shambles. I urge our lawmakers to give Christians and other religious minorities in Iraq, like the Yazidis, the resources they need to return home. May we show the world that we have not forgotten them and the United States still stands up for the vulnerable and for those under threat within our borders and beyond.

I would like to leave you today with some compelling video that we gathered of the destruction as well as the rebirth of the Christian communities in northern Iraq. They speak for themselves.

Thank you.

[Video.]

[The prepared statement of Ms. Ashburn follows:]

Chairman Smith, Ranking Member Bass, Members of the Subcommittee.
Good afternoon.

Thank you for inviting me to appear before you today.

In April of this year, I set out with a team from my network, EWTN, to report on the plight of
Christians and other religious minorities in the northern Iraqi city of Erbil and the Nineveh Plain,
to the north and east of Mosul. My team included the following members of my staff: Susanna
Pinto, Paul Fifield and Tom Haller. We knew that these groups had suffered genocide, as the
U.S. State Department recognized in March of 2016, and we had read about their harrowing
experiences. But we were not prepared for the death and destruction we were about to witness.

Christians in Iraq are on the brink of extinction. And I saw that grim reality first hand.

My visit to the town of Batnaya in northern Iraq embodies the experience of Christians in the
region. Islamic State forces controlled the Christian enclave for two years before Kurdish
fighters pushed them out in November 2016. As I toured the devastated town, I could hear
explosions from the fighting in Mosul, about 15 miles away.

What I saw was absolute evil in the form of devastation and destruction. ISIS has flattened
ninety percent of Batnaya. The village literally looks like an earthquake struck. And the danger
is not over. There are signs everywhere warning of IEDs and booby traps.

The Catholic Church – in the center of the town – is still standing, only because ISIS used it as
its command center. But it has been severely damaged and desecrated. A statue of the Virgin
Mary is decapitated, and other statues are smashed to bits. The face of Jesus has been ripped
from paintings and bullet holes mark the place where a Cross once was. Every Christian symbol
I could see has been defaced or obliterated. I couldn't hold back my tears.

In a nearby graveyard, Christian headstones are uprooted or desecrated. Even a final resting
place was not safe from the fury of the Islamic State.

I spoke with a Christian grandmother and her daughter, who had fled the jihadists' onslaught
with their family. They sobbed while looking at the damage to their home. Their whole life was
there, and they want desperately to return, but they have no money to rebuild. Still, the
daughter's husband climbed to the roof and tied a makeshift cross to a metal rod sticking out of
it.

Similar scenes can be seen in other Christian towns in the area, including Qaraqosh, which was
freed from Islamic State in October 2016 but suffered appalling damage. Many Christians in
northern Iraq feel abandoned in the aftermath of the U.S.-led war that toppled Saddam Hussein.
During my visit, headlines in the U.S. focused on the gas attack in neighboring Syria and two
horrifying church bombings in Egypt, which killed dozens and were claimed by Islamic State.
But events in Iraq seldom get as much attention. The American public seems to have moved on.

Despite having survived genocide, Christians in Northern Iraq want to go back to their homeland.

In Batnaya on Palm Sunday, I witnessed a crowd of Christians return for the day for Mass and a procession. At the church, a priest, aided by volunteers, had spent weeks cleaning up. As the priest conducted the service in Aramaic – the language of Jesus Christ - the altar behind him was still covered in rubble. The congregation erected a huge metal cross where the altar used to be, decorated with burning votive candles, and they had placed palm branches on the crosses defaced by Islamic State—a small symbol of hope over hate.

The United States is the only nation in the world that can provide concrete aid to rebuild the community that I saw in shambles. I urge our lawmakers to give Christians and other religious minorities in Iraq and Syria the resources they need to return home. May we show the world that we have not forgotten them and the United States still stand up for the vulnerable and those under threat, within our borders - or beyond.

I'd like to leave you today with some compelling video that we gathered of the destruction as well as the rebirth of the Christian communities in Northern Iraq. They speak for themselves. Thank you.

Lauren Ashburn
Anchor & Managing Editor, EWTN News Nightly

Mr. SMITH. Ms. Ashburn, thank you very much for your excellent testimony, for bringing back for all of us to see those very vivid images, not only of the devastation but of the hope reflected in those and, you could tell, in the hearts and minds of the people that were being interviewed.

I would now ask that Mr. Rasche begin his testimony. I would point out that when Mr. Rasche testified almost a year ago to the day, September 22nd, before us he said, "It is no exaggeration to say without these private donors"—and he pointed out the Knights of Columbus, Aid to the Church in Need, Caritas of Italy, had provided some $26 million at that point—"the situation for Christians in northern Iraq would have collapsed and the vast majority of these families would, without question, have already joined the refugee diaspora now destabilizing the Middle East and Europe."

He pointed out that throughout the entirety of the crisis since August 2014, other than an initial supply of tents and tarps, the Christian community in Iraq has received nothing in aid from the U.S. aid agencies or the United Nations. Which I found appalling at the time which is why, again, this is the 10th hearing in a series that we have had. We had administration witnesses appear. We pleaded with them to provide that aid. They always say they would look into it. And then nothing happened.

Now, we do have legislation as you know, H.R. 390, which will make sure that the job gets done. Frank Wolf has made a number of very important recommendations, including that point person to really be the catalyst to make sure that the Christians and the Yazidis and other minorities are cared for.

But, again, I look forward to your testimony now, especially in light of you having lived this. You have been the IDP person. It must be agonizing to know that the resources should be there and have not been.

STATEMENT OF MR. STEPHEN RASCHE, LEGAL COUNSEL, DIRECTOR OF INTERNATIONALLY DISPLACED PERSONS ASSISTANCE, CHALDEAN CATHOLIC ARCHDIOCESE OF ERBIL

Mr. RASCHE. Thank you, Mr. Chairman, for giving me the opportunity to come back and speak to you again.

Again, my name is Stephen Rasche. And I come to you from Erbil in northern Iraq, but most recently to the towns that Lauren—from the towns that Lauren's video has just shown to you. The towns of Batnaya and Teleskov are where I spend most of my time these days, along with the other Christian towns out in the Iraqi sector.

In my work in Erbil I serve on the staff of the Catholic Archdiocese of Erbil. And in that context I serve as legal counsel for external affairs, the Director of IDP Resettlement Programs, which includes the Nineveh Reconstruction Project.

Since 2014, the Archdiocese of Erbil has provided almost all the medical care, food, shelter, and education for the more than 100,000 Christians that fled ISIS, as well as many Yazidis and Muslims who are also in our care. Mr. Chairman, I wish I could tell you that in the 12 months that followed since my last appearance here that our pleas have been heard and that our plight had found relief. But as I speak before you now, I regret to say that we have still yet to receive any form of meaningful aid from the U.S. Government.

While we have found the political appointees much more willing to help us since January, the fact is that even after the better part of a year they have been unable to move the bureaucracy to take meaningful action. Last month, Secretary of State Rex Tillerson reaffirmed that Iraq's religious minorities were the victims of genocide. But even that declaration, combined with the statutary mandate—statutory mandate to aid these communities with funds allocated for fiscal year 2017 by Congress in the Consolidated Appropriations Act for May, has been insufficient to create action on the part of these agencies.

The fiscal year ended days ago, with these agencies continuing to shirk their statutory obligations. Still no aid has been provided to the imperiled Christian minority.

These humanitarian principles are intended to prevent aid from being used to punish or reward religious, national, or racial groups. It was and is incomprehensible to us that these principles have been interpreted and applied to prohibit intentionally helping religious and ethnic minority communities to survive genocide. Interestingly, these principles were waived last month when the Department of State's Bureau for Population, Refugees, and Migration provided 32 million in emergency humanitarian assistance to the Rohingya Muslims, a religious minority in Burma.

As an American, I am proud when my country responds to a humanitarian crisis, but this action begs the question of why the State Department, which has distributed over $220 million [1] in humanitarian assistance in Iraq since 2014, has consistently ignored the dire needs of the persecuted minorities in Iraq.

Given this, H.R. 390, the Genocide Relief Act, is a vital lifeline we have desperately needed for months. The House of Representatives passed it unanimously on June the 6th, and the Senate Foreign Relations Committee passed it unanimously on September 19th, yet still it sits in the Senate. We hope that they will consider our existential plight, and that time is short fo us, and make it law soon.

Mr. Chairman, had we received any kind of proper assistance from the U.S. Government for the nearly 100,000 displaced Christians in our care who had to flee ISIS, we would by now have been able to resettle the vast majority of them back into their homes in the recovered towns of Nineveh. Instead, our pool of private donors and already limited funds have dwindled. We had hoped to use these resources for the return of displaced Christians. Instead, we had to repurpose much of these funds for the ongoing humanitarian needs of these same displaced people.

We are, thus, faced with the excruciating decision of whether to continue keeping our people housed and fed in temporary shelters in Erbil, or return them to their destroyed towns with only the barest funds to rebuild in Nineveh.

I will not repeat what you read into the record earlier regarding the Nineveh Reconstruction Committee except to say we des-

---

[1] This figure is for FY 2017 only. Since 2014 the amount is over $896 million.

perately need your help, and we certainly thank you for your support in it.

To close up here I would say to you we are now caught in a situation where we are fully exposed and at risk, and finding ourselves at a critical, historical inflection point. While status reports from the UNDP work in Nineveh purport to show real progress in the Christian majority towns, on the ground we see little evidence of it. Work projects are in most cases cosmetic in nature, and much of that cynically so. Completed school rehabilitation projects in Teleskov, and Batnaya, and Bartella take the form of one thin coat of painting on the exterior surface walls, with freshly stenciled UNICEF logos every 30 feet.

Meanwhile, inside the rooms remain untouched and unusable. There is no water. There is no power. There is no furniture.

I have pictures that I can show you of these worksites later on in the question and answer period that give a pretty clear picture of what the nature of the work is there.

One more thing that I would like to note is in the UNDP reports claiming to show the work being done in areas in which religious minorities are the majority, prominently list work in the formerly Christian town of Telkayf. A copy of this report has been distributed to this committee. Mr. Chairman, there are no more Christians in Telkayf. They were forced from this town by acts of genocide, crimes against humanity, and war crimes. ISIS was firmly in control of this town until last fall, and many of its Sunni Arab residents remain.

Many of those residents who openly welcomed ISIS while simultaneously engaging in forced and violent expulsion of the Christian majority are still there.

Telkayf has also been chosen as a settlement site for the families of slain ISIS fighters. As such, 100 percent of the work being done in this town benefits the Sunni Arab residents of the town, and there is no consideration anywhere in U.N. aid planning for the displaced Christians, who now depend wholly upon the church and private sources for their survival.

So, what can be done in all of this? As Congressman Wolf has said earlier, first, the Senate can pass H.R. 390 without further delay.

Second, the proposal of the Nineveh Reconstruction Committee, now sitting with USAID Administrator Mark Green, can be swiftly approved and implemented.

Third, again echoing the comments of Congressman Wolf, since the agencies so far have ignored the statutory obligation to care for genocide-targeted communities, as Congress has mandated, we would strongly urge that Congress urge this administration to appoint an interagency coordinator empowered to oversee and solve this issue.

Thank you, Mr. Chairman. I look forward to your questions.

[The prepared statement of Mr. Rasche follows:]

**Statement by
Stephen M. Rasche, Esq.
Legal Counsel & Director of IDP Resettlement Programs,
Chaldean Catholic Archdiocese of Erbil
Kurdistan Region, Iraq
House Foreign Affairs Committee, Subcommittee on Africa, Global Health,
Global Human Rights, and International Organizations
A hearing on "Atrocities in Iraq and Syria: Relief for Survivors and
Accountability for Perpetrators"**

Tuesday, October 3, 2017

Thank you Mr. Chairman and members of the Committee for allowing me to speak to you on behalf of the persecuted Christians of Northern Iraq.

My name is Stephen Rasche, and I presently reside in Erbil, capital of the Kurdistan Region of Iraq, and home to what is presently the largest viable Christian community in Iraq. In Erbil I serve on the staff of the Chaldean Catholic Archdiocese of Erbil. Within that context I serve as legal counsel for external affairs, Director of IDP Resettlement Programs, including the Nineveh Reconstruction Project, and Vice Chancellor of the Catholic University in Erbil.

Since 2014, the Archdiocese of Erbil has provided almost all the medical care, food, shelter and education for the more than 100,000 Christians who had to flee ISIS, as well as aid to some Yazidis and Muslims.

Just over one year ago I testified here on the Capitol Hill before the Helsinki Commission regarding the critical need for help to the displaced Christians of northern Iraq. I specifically laid out the ways in which the Christians were being shut out from institutional aid, such as that distributed through the United Nations. I explained as well the critical role being played by the private aid community, without whom the Christians of rorthern Iraq would have by then already perished. I asked that the US Government hear our pleas for help, and warned that without this help, the Christians of the Nineveh Plain could very well disappear.

I wish that I could tell you that in the twelve months that followed that our pleas were heard, and that our plight has found relief. But as I speak before you now, I regret to say that we have still yet to receive any form of meaningful aid from the US Government.

Over the past three years, we repeatedly approached the State Department and US Agency for International Development in Iraq and in Washington, DC to see if they would be willing to fund our humanitarian and rebuilding aid programs. We explained the needs on-the-ground were outpacing private funding and help from governments like the United States was needed to enable these communities to survive.

While we have found the political appointees much more willing to help us since January, the fact is that even after the better part of a year, they have been unable to move the bureaucracy to take meaningful action.

Even in the new administration, career individuals at these agencies have continued to state that they are only concerned with individuals, not communities. They have asserted that directing assistance to particular religious or ethnic communities would be "discrimination" and a "violation of humanitarian principles," even if these communities had been targeted for genocide and assistance was being directed to them to prevent their destruction. We were also told their own administrative interpretation of humanitarian principles superseded U.S. appropriations law that specifically stated that 2017 "International Assistance and Migration and Refugee Assistance shall be made available for humanitarian assistance for vulnerable and persecuted religious minorities, including victims of genocide designated by the Secretary of State." Last month Secretary of State Rex Tillerson reaffirmed that Iraq's religious minorities were the victims of genocide. But even that declaration, combined with the statutory mandate to aid these communities with funds allocated for FY 2017 by Congress in the Consolidated Appropriations Act from May, has been insufficient to create action on the part of these agencies. The fiscal year ended days ago, with these agencies continuing to shirk their statutory obligations. Still no aid has been provided to the imperiled Christian minority.

These humanitarian principles are intended to prevent aid from being used to punish or reward religious, national or racial groups. It was and is incomprehensible to us that these principles have been interpreted and applied to prohibit intentionally helping religious and ethnic minority communities survive genocide. Interestingly, these "principles" were waived last month when the Department of State's Bureau for Population, Refugees and Migration provided $32 million in emergency humanitarian assistance to the Rohingya Muslims – a religious minority in Burma. As an American I am proud when my country responds to a humanitarian crisis, but this action begs the question of why the State Department, which has distributed over $220 million in humanitarian assistance in Iraq since 2014, has consistently ignored the dire needs of persecuted minorities in Iraq.

In Iraq, the Christian community has been formally named by the U.S. Government as the targets of genocide. Congress has mandated by statute that communities under such a genocide designation must receive humanitarian funding. And yet, we have received nothing, while another group, without a formal genocide designation or statutory mandate, has received tens of millions of dollars.

We must ask, why the discrepancy? Why is there not a common principle here when it comes to religious minority communities in distress?

As such, HR 390, the Iraq and Syria Genocide Relief and Accountability Act, is a vital lifeline we have desperately needed for months. The House of Representatives passed it unanimously on June 6 and the Senate Foreign Relations Committee passed it unanimously September 19. Yet, it still sits in the Senate. We hope that they will consider our existential plight and that time is short for us and make it law soon.

We have explained that as victims of genocide, Christian settlements suffered comparatively more physical damage than others specifically because of their religious identity for the purpose of eradicating any vestige of their previous existence in Iraq. Christians have seen the lowest rate of return among all Iraqi citizens displaced by the war. East Mosul, for example, has seen over 90% of its majority-Muslim people return home, while the nearby Nineveh Plain, the ancient homeland of Iraq's Christian communities, has seen only about 20% of its people return though these lands were liberated months earlier. This deep sectarian-based return gap reflects the unique large scale and deliberate destruction of Christian towns, but it also reflects the refusal of US aid agencies, and their implementing partners, to include these victimized communities in their humanitarian and rebuilding programs.

Had we received any kind of proper assistance from the US government for the nearly 100,000 displaced Christians in our care who had to flee ISIS, we would by now have been able to resettle the vast majority of them back into their homes in the recovered towns of Nineveh.

Instead, our pool of private donors and already limited funds have dwindled. We had hoped to use these resources for the return of displaced Christians. Instead, we had to repurpose some of these funds for the ongoing humanitarian needs of these same displaced people, including food.

We were thus faced with the excruciating decision of whether to continue keeping our people housed and fed in temporary shelters in Erbil, or return them to their destroyed towns with only the barest funds to rebuild in Nineveh. The towns of Nineveh that were Christian before ISIS are facing new pressures of forced demographic changes, financed by an Iran that seeks to build a bridgehead to the Mediterranean Sea through these lands. So, earlier this year, in response to growing calls by Christian IDPs to return home, we began to support the return of these Christians and rebuilding of their homes and towns through the Nineveh Reconstruction Committee.

The Nineveh Reconstruction Committee (NRC) is a formal, ecumenical partnership between the three largest Christian churches in Iraq: The Chaldean Catholic Church, Syriac Catholic Church and Syriac Orthodox Church. As such, it represents in a unified manner the overwhelming majority of Christians still in Iraq. Its Nineveh Sustainable Return Program seeks to promote sustainable returns by repairing 9,000 homes ISIS damaged or destroyed, removing war rubble to make these towns safe, and giving these communities a voice in the rebuilding of their communities. In a display of transatlantic solidarity, Aid to the Church in Need in Europe and the Knights of Columbus in the United States partnered to launch this $29.5 million initiative. With a combined $7 million in funding from these charities, and with additional support from the Hungarian government, we have already repaired 2,254 homes, revived two towns and helped more than 11,000 Christian and other religious minorities return home. Given a fair opportunity to return home, the Christians go home.

Let me be very clear on this point. There is no truth to the argument that Christians in Iraq don't want or need U.S. government assistance. We have been seeking it for years, and continue to seek in a unified way under the collaborative banner of the NRC.

On September 15, this group's sister organization, the Nineveh Reconstruction Committee USA, of which I am President, submitted to the US Agency for International Development a proposal seeking more than $22 million in funds to build upon the tangible progress we are making to enable families to return. Without such additional funding, however, this initiative will end before it is completed, jeopardizing the very survival of the Iraqi Christian community.

Today, as I speak to you, we are caught fully exposed and at-risk, finding ourselves at a critical historical inflection point, foreign aid decisions over which will determine whether Christianity, and religious pluralism – vital to the US national interest and regional security – will survive in Iraq at all. A depopulated Nineveh Plain, control over which is already fueling competing and sectarian-based claims, is a recipe for more conflict. We are out of funds, our people are trying to return to their homes, the backlash from the Kurdish Referendum has created enormous uncertainty, and our people still have yet to receive any meaningful help from the US or its main implementing partner in Iraq, the United Nations, despite billions in US aid dollars already spent on the Iraq and Syria crises.

The UN Development Programme administers the Funding Facility for Stabilization which is the main instrument through which the US Government seeks to promote post-ISIS stabilization, rehabilitation and political stability in Iraq. The US Agency for International Development has so far spent or allocated all of its funding for stabilization in Iraq, over $265 million so far, through this mechanism. While status reports from UNDP work in Nineveh purport to show real progress in the Christian majority towns, on the ground we see little evidence of it. Work projects are in most cases cosmetic in nature, and much of that cynically so. "Completed" school rehabilitation projects in Teleskov and Batnaya take the form of one thin coat of painting of the exterior surface walls, with freshly stenciled UNICEF logos every 30 feet. Meanwhile inside, the rooms remain untouched and unusable: there is no water, no power, and no furniture. These pictures taken 10 days ago give an example. Bear in mind that these are government schools, which were due to open today.

Moreover, UNDP reports claiming to show the work being done in areas in which religious minorities are the majority prominently list work done in the formerly Christian town of Telkayf. A copy of this report has been distributed to this committee. Mr. Chairman, there are no more Christians in Telkayf. They were forced from this town by acts of genocide, crimes against humanity and war crimes. ISIS was firmly in control of this town until last fall and many of its Sunni Arab residents remained. Many of those residents, who openly welcomed ISIS while simultaneously engaging in the forced and violent expulsion of the majority Christians, are still there.

Telkayf has also been chosen as a settlement site for the families of slain ISIS fighters. As such, 100 percent of the work being done in this town benefits the Sunni Arab residents of the town, and there is no consideration anywhere in UN aid planning for the displaced Christians, who now depend wholly upon the Church and private sources for their survival. This is well over 10,000 families. That such a representation could be made in the UNDP report, without even the barest attempt at an explanatory note, shows clearly the profound depth of disconnect between representation and reality. In effect, US taxpayers are financing the spoils of genocide.

So what can be done? First, the Senate can pass HR 390 without further delay, thereby returning it to the House for a final vote so it can be sent to the President for his signature and implementation.

Second, the proposal of the Nineveh Reconstruction Committee, now sitting with USAID Administrator Ambassador Mark Green, can be swiftly approved and implemented. It embodies the collective efforts and good will of the people on the ground in Iraq and their supporters around the world, including many Members of Congress, to refuse to submit to ISIS's campaign of hatred and deny it an ideological victory in Iraq. It is also good aid policy. It offers the US Government a unique opportunity to have a major impact on Iraq's democratic future and prevent a key ISIS goal of cleansing Iraq of its ancient Christians from becoming fact. It would build upon on an existing success story and do so more cost-effectively, without waste and fraud, give Iraq's minorities a say in the rebuilding of their own future, and breathe new life and hope in a stable and prosperous Iraq.

Third, since the agencies have so far ignored the statutory obligation to care for genocide-targeted communities as Congress mandated, I would suggest that Congress urge this Administration to appoint an interagency coordinator empowered to oversee and solve this issue.

These actions taken together can immediately begin to demonstrate the effectiveness of a new aid paradigm which directly empowers and benefits the most vulnerable communities in Iraq and prevent the extermination of this ancient community.

Thank you Mr. Chairman I look forward to your questions.

Mr. GARRETT [presiding]. The Chair recognizes the gentlewoman from Hawaii, Ms. Gabbard.

So I would recognize myself. It is quite a luxury to be sitting in the chairman's seat where I don't have to worry about my 5 minutes as much.

It is really an honor to be here in front of you all today. Congressman Wolf and I have known each other sort of bouncing off one and another for years, but I have always been a big admirer and respecter of the work he has done.

There are a couple things that stood out to me today as I sort of took some notes and then bounced a lot of this against my own perspective. I had the honor of serving in the United States military for a number of years, and in so doing served right in between IFOR and SFOR as it served in Bosnia to implement the Dayton Peace Accords and put a halt to the Bosnian genocide.

Did a little bit of quick leg work and saw that, at the time, that was considered to be the most costly genocidal act perpetrated by some, particularly and certainly on the European continent since World War II. And the death toll was 100,000. I think we are well beyond that as it relates to Yazidis and Christians, in Syria and Iraq specifically, but in the greater region in particular. And it strikes me as noteworthy that, for example, in Turkey the Christian population of the nation in 1914 was 19 percent. And then following the First World War and the Armenian genocide it dropped to 2.5 percent in 1927, to today where it's at 0.2 percent, two-tenths of 1 percent.

And we see the same thing in the area. So, about 10 days I got off an airplane from Khartoum in the Republic of the Sudan where just yesterday morning I was able to meet at the airport the last two of nine Christian refugees who we extracted from that country, the two patriarchs of these families having spent 18 months of the last 24 in prison, essentially for providing foodstuffs and medicines to religious minorities in the south of that country. So I have tried very hard to respect the legacy of folks like the chairman of this subcommittee Mr. Smith, and Congressman Wolf, and take that message and the opportunity to help afforded by the privilege of serving this body abroad.

Having said that, let me differentiate, as an admirer of Jefferson and someone who considers himself a Christian, although the degree to which I am a good one is probably to be determined by an arbiter greater than myself, between my role as a Member of Congress and my faith, and that is that my job is to not enforce my faith and tenets on others but to be an arbiter of that which is within the purview of government at the Federal level in the United States to the ¼₃₅th fraction that I command responsibility for in the one-half of two legislative bodies and one of three legislative branches.

So, I say these things not as a Christian but as an American who has some responsibility vested in him by the citizens of the Fifth District of Virginia.

There is no excuse for this. There is no excuse for a nation that's sought actively to put itself at the forefront of global justice and security for generations to stand idly by while one group of individuals is targeted, whether they be Yazidis, or Christians, or Jews, or Muslims, or what have you. And the silence is deafening. And those who choose not to act, I believe, and I will step out of my congressional shoes for a moment, will be held to account once again by authority far greater than that which is manifest in this body.

So, Congressman Wolf called for bold action. And, obviously, we're a co-patron of H.R. 390. I want to commend the 47 co-patrons, and specifically Members Schiff, Cardenas, Slaughter, Lipinski, Vargas, Eshoo, and Sherman for being Democrats on that bill. There is no reason this should be partisan. And my friend and colleague with whom I have worked, Ms. Gabbard from Hawaii, in joining us. I hope that this is something that should reach, and believe, a bipartisan consensus that holding people to account for acts that penalize human beings by virtue of a value structure that does nothing to hurt others aside from themselves would be something that we could unite upon, and perhaps demonstrate to the American people that there is some commonality in values shared in this body, and that we can work together to advance good causes.

So, I say that not to cast aspersions or throw barbs, but to generally and sincerely invite folks to get on board. And we will work as an office later today to put out invitations for others to join us in this bill.

But I move back to what I said, that two sets of words struck me. First was Congressman Wolf's call for bold action. Beyond H.R. 390 I would invite you to articulate what sort of action that would be and what we need to be doing. One thing I know is that I don't know everything. And that when you are sitting here you need to know a little bit about so many things that it is hard to know a lot about anything. So, you have been able to step away after years of wonderful service and sort of focus. What else do we need to be doing.

Mr. WOLF. The President ought to appoint one person, he or she that has his authority. And they ought to be invited to the White House, whether it be the Rose Garden, to do the same thing that President Bush did with regard to former Senator John Danforth. When the Sudanese issue was unraveling, President Bush invited former Senator John Danforth. He came to the White house. They stood in the Rose Garden. It was the day before 9/11. I was there. And he stood between President Bush on one side and Secretary Powell on the other side. And the President made it clear, this was his person who was going to solve this problem.

President Trump ought to do the same thing. The President needs to be engaged. So, he should invite whoever that person is to the White House and where the appointment would be made. On one side would be President Trump, the other side Secretary Tillerson. That will send a message to the government, to all employees, to the Congress, to the world, but also to the Yazidi community. We went out and met with the Yazidi religious leadership. They are suffering. They haven't seen anything to help them. And 3,000 girls are currently held by them. And so that one thing wold do more than anything else.

And then from there, personnel would do policy, you could begin to change some of the policies.

Mr. GARRETT. What was the title——

Mr. WOLF. If it doesn't get done by the end of the year, it is going to be over.

Mr. GARRETT. So that Senator Danforth's title was what? I do not recall.

Mr. WOLF. It was called Envoy for Peace in Sudan. He was the one that negotiated the north/south peace agreement that led to the breaking up of the Sudan whereby Southern Sudan became a separate country.

Mr. GARRETT. Special Envoy for Oppressed Religious Minorities?

Mr. WOLF. Call it whatever makes the administration feel comfortable. But personnel is policy. You want to put the right person who really cares, who weeps, who really is committed to this. And that person can, I think, solve the problem.

Mr. GARRETT. I got some ideas on who might fill that role well. But I won't, I won't editorialize.

The other thing that struck me, there were two things. Again, Congressman Wolf's testimony. Again, I invite you to reach out. I called. You called back. And we need to close that loop because I hope I might be able to learn some things from you.

But the other thing that really struck me was Ms. Shireen's words through her interpreter, "and then I was sold." "And then they sold me." It is 2017; right? I mean, we have problems in this country, to be sure, that are worthy of attention and addressing. The fact that that sort of activity still occurs on this Earth and that our Government has been largely silent and, candidly, in the interest of honesty, in a vacuum which we were pivotal in creating, it can't be justified.

So, again, I invite members of the community to reach out to our office, and specifically with concrete ideas of what we can do. We can sort of exchange rhetorical flourish about injustice all day. I am with you. But the challenge is, if you want to be a Ph.D. you have to know something about—or everything about something. If you want to do this work you have got to know something about everything. So I need you all.

Having said that, does anybody on the panel feel that there is anything that they would like to add to the discourse that they missed the opportunity for? Sort of an open invitation.

I would then yield to my colleague and friend from Hawaii Ms. Gabbard.

Ms. GABBARD. Thank you very much. Thanks to you all for your leadership and for being here.

Ms. Shireen, it is nice to see you again. I am glad that you are here and continuing to share your story and the story of many of your Yazidi brothers and sisters whose voices are not being heard.

My question is for Ms. Shireen about a comment that's very important that you made regarding that even if and when ISIS is defeated in Iraq, the ideology that has driven their genocide against religious minorities remains. How do you see that manifesting itself?

And as the different communities begin to put the pieces back together in their lives, who can best influence these groups of people to defeat that ideology?

Ms. SHIREEN. Thank you for your question. I think as we have seen as a terrorist attacked us, not only ISIS, but before ISIS there were other groups that attacked Yazidi villages. There was one explosion actually in one of the Yazidi towns in 2007. It was one of the biggest ones in Iraq in the recent decade or so.

Seeing that, after going back home it is hard for Yazidis to trust the same forces, the same leadership that was supposedly protecting us and left us within ISIS. So it is hard for the Yazidi community. They hope that the United States will take the leadership and make sure that security is provided for those religious minorities, not only Yazidis but others too.

You know, so even with the liberated areas, for those families that are going back to their homes many are exploding, too, from the mines that ISIS left behind. As you saw in the video, Yazidi areas are not much different than Christian areas. They are basically destroyed. So people are not sure where to go.

Just like how they destroyed the churches in Christian towns, they destroyed all of our temples. People are scared. They are traumatized to go back again unless they have some sort of security, they have some sort of guarantees. But some people don't have any other choices because they have been living in the camps for years now. And some just go back.

And going back home is not easy because now the Yazidi homeland is divided between all different groups. It is the PMF, the Shia militia on one side, the Peshmerga on the other side. The Kurdistan Workers' Party (PKK) has taken a portion. And the Patriotic Union of Kurdistan (PUK) is there. And due to the political competition, not much can be done. Yazidis themselves can't do much for themselves while that political competition is ongoing.

It is true that our areas were neglected before ISIS. We lived a simple life. It was not perfect but we were happy. But when ISIS came they destroyed everything. They destroyed, they shattered our families. They killed some and they abducted others. So, all we ask is to be able to live safely in our homes with dignity.

And with that, I thank you very much for your time and for the opportunity to speak.

Ms. GABBARD. Thank you.

Lastly, Mr. Rasche, you know we have heard a number of times over the last several months from different officials within the State Department about this $100 million in assistance that they claim has been disbursed in Iraq for the religious and ethnic minority groups, including the Yazidis, Christians, and Shia. However, this number has never been quantified for us about how it has been delivered, how it has been delivered, what kind of impact it has made. And they have not provided an explanation about why this number dates all the way back to 2008.

With a year on the ground you have got a close pulse on what is happening there. If you can provide any real view on this statement that the State Department continues to make?

Mr. RASCHE. Well, I think the—you mentioned, rightly so, that they had to stretch back to 2008 in order to get that number which I think is indicative of how far the reaches have to go in order to make it appear that things are really happening.

I can simply say that on the ground we don't see it. And we tell people this. And when we tell them, we don't see this, we don't see this money that you say is being spent here, the response is generally, "Well, it is being sent, it is being spent. We have a report that says so."

And this is the, this is a common response that we get. And, you know, it puts us in a difficult position because, sure, we don't want to spend our time bashing the U.N. We would like to be singing their praises. But at the same time, we are responsible for taking care of these people. And we see this work, it is objectively not happening the way it is being described.

And I have just come back from a similar visit to the U.K. where we spoke with the DFID minister, their equivalent of the USAID. And they are having the same issue there trying to match the granularity of reports with what people are actually seeing on the ground.

And so it is a common problem. I don't think it is just unique here to the U.S. And it has to do with the fact that the verification of this work is being left to the people who do the work. And that is not a system that you accept anywhere. And why we accept it in a situation where we are spending hundreds of millions of dollars and where people's lives are fundamentally at risk based upon the outcomes, it is, this is the heart of it.

And as Congressman Wolf pointed out in his trip over there, you can't miss the disconnect that is going on between the reporting and what is actually happening on the ground. And the solution for that is better reporting by your own people. You cannot let the people doing the work report on what a great job they are doing because they are doing a great job always.

Ms. GABBARD. Thank you.

Mr. GARRETT. I will yield back to the chair in a moment. But right now I have the microphone.

So, there are a couple of observations I want to make real quickly and then thank you all. But, again, there is a sincere and literal invitation for each and every one of you to reach out to our office to the extent that there are actual, literal, concrete measures to be taken that are within the purview of this body. This is what I know is that I don't know what I don't know.

You know, I see cameras in this room, and that is important because I think the world doesn't begin to grasp the scope. We spoke earlier of the Bosnian genocide. If you look at the displacement numbers externally, we are essentially the population of Wisconsin, to bring it home to the American viewing public. If you look at IDPs along with externally displaced individuals, you are at the population of Michigan. And that is a number that is sort of nebulous.

The one thing that we have said repeatedly in this committee and this subcommittee is that the 5+ million externally displaced individuals have one thing in common, and that is that they don't want to be displaced; right? And that our job as a nation isn't to advocate on behalf of a specific faith, but it certainly is to advocate on behalf of human beings. So we should do a better job of that.

I wonder in sort of the rhetorical sense, Mr. Rasche, just how much money of that $100 million is pay-to-play. Unfortunately, in this part of the world if we don't keep a close eye on where the money goes a lot of palms get greased before the assets ever hit the ground. And I would submit that as good stewards, hopefully, our tax dollars, that we shouldn't allocate funds that we can't assure are going to be spent responsibly because ultimately what we end up doing is enriching the very people who perpetuated the atrocities that we seek to correct.

And, finally, I will say this: During my time in the Balkans I noticed a number of churches destroyed and a number of mosques destroyed. The common theme was that wherever there was a mosque destroyed there was a sign, white with green print, in multiple languages that said, "This mosque being refurbished by the benevolent people of the Kingdom of Saudi Arabia." And there was no counter. Now, again, it is not the role of the United States Government to build churches, but it is the role of the United States Government to advocate on behalf of oppressed minorities, particularly in regions where we have created circumstances that might have helped perpetuate that oppression.

So, I hope that you all will continue to do the good work that you do, that the American and global public will start to understand the scope and scale here, simply in terms of death toll of Yazidis and Christians who are in a circumstance that is twice that, based on the best numbers I can find, of the Bosnian genocide. And that doesn't begin to address millions of people who will perhaps, unfortunately, never see their homes again.

So, again, thank you for your time. Thank you, Mr. Chair, for the gavel. And with that I will yield back.

Mr. SMITH [presiding]. Thank you very much, Mr. Garrett. Thank you for taking the gavel.

I had to speak on H.R. 36, the Pain-Capable Unborn Child Protection Act, and my slot had come up. So I missed your oral presentation, Mr. Rasche, but I did read it. And was very moved by the detail that you have provided in this important testimony.

So let me ask you, begin by asking you a couple questions about it. I would just point out for the record that when we held hearing after hearing, and you testified at two of them, we kept getting told by the Obama administration while we were looking into it "we may get back, we will get back." And they never did.

And then when I decided I have got to go look myself as to why this, this reluctance, this gross indifference to the Christians and the Yazidis who were working, and really surviving side-by-side in Erbil. We went around Christmastime. As a matter of fact the trip itself was postponed several times because of an inability on the part of the State Department to accommodate it. So I said even if we come on Christmas Day, we are coming. So, 2 days before Christmas we were there.

When we got there we were told that an IDP camp that was about 10 minutes away from the consulate offices in Erbil, which had not been visited, until we were coming, by State Department people, I was told it was too dangerous to go there. And I said, "Are you kidding me?" I mean, "Is there a personal threat directed against me and my delegation as to why we shouldn't go there?" take threat assessments very seriously.

But they said, "No."

And I said, "Well, I have been in refugee camps"—maybe not as many as Congressman Frank Wolf—but all over the world, in Darfur and all over the world.

So we went. And Archbishop Warda drove. I sat to his side. We got there and we were met by very, very joy-filled people full of faith and hope, people who wondered why the United States Government was not helping them. And then we heard hundreds of children singing Christmas carols. And then I really felt threatened, you know, little 5-, 6-, 7-, 8-year-olds singing Christmas carols a couple days before Christmas.

It was an absurdity because, again, they had been, in my opinion, grossly indifferent to the plight and the needs that we had raised—and I am not the only one that raised it—so consistently over the course of several years.

You point out, Mr. Rasche, that the excruciating decision, as you put it, whether continuing to keep people housed and fed versus the return issue. You point out that the lack of funding and other challenges mean that about 80, 90 percent of the majority Muslim people have returned home, whereas only about 20 percent of the Christians. And I think that that tells a story in and of itself.

As Ms. Ashburn pointed out in her testimony, not only were Christians killed and raped and mutilated, but churches were booby trapped, desecrated, statues of the Blessed Mother decapitated, all in a genocidal campaign against Christians as well as against Yazidis and others. But the focus numbers-wise obviously is toward the Christian churches.

If you would just explain further this request that you have made. You did explain it somewhat in your testimony. How much money were you able to glean from the Knights of Columbus and others which was absolutely the bridge that kept people alive? And, again, the people I met with we went all over that refugee camp, or IDP camp I should say, they were all very thin. They looked relatively healthy. But they could use a lot more in medicines, food, shelter. They were cramped in very, very small quarters.

And I know you have made a major effort to try to get them placed in better living accommodations. That is part of the plan that you have crafted so skillfully. But if you could just talk a little bit more about the Nineveh Reconstruction Committee, which you pointed out is doing very good work with the ecumenical partnership between the three largest Christian churches: The Chaldean Catholic Church, Syriac Catholic Church, and the Orthodox Church as well.

Mr. RASCHE. Sure, Mr. Chairman. Just real quickly then, in terms of the humanitarian aid over the past year, that, that aid came to us almost exclusively from the Aid to Church in Need and the Knights of Columbus. There were other church-related groups that did continue to assist us. But in this last year for housing, food, medicine it was all church-related donations that kept us going.

As we move into the situation now with the towns liberated and the people going into the fourth year in their displaced status we had to make a decision, would we continue supporting them in a displaced status or help to move them back into their homes? Ideally, we would have liked to have made a transition where they could rebuild their community and then move in as it was rebuilt.

But because we had no funding to do this from anybody we had to short circuit it. And so we ended our housing program and told people, unfortunately, we have to begin moving you back whether your towns are ready for it or not, whether there is water there, whether there is power there, whether your building and your home is inhabitable or not. And we will be there beside you and do everything we can to make these houses habitable, and make these towns safe and operating as soon as we can. But it is clearly not the, not the best choice.

We were helped tremendously in this project by the, by the Government of Hungary who showed—and of course the politics in the EU are quite complicated on this, and we don't look to make any judgment one way or another on that, except to say that the Government of Hungary, when nobody else would, stepped forward and provided us with the funds to save one town. It was the first town, the town of Teleskov. And it gave the people tremendous hope across the spectrum of the Christian communities hoping to return to Nineveh that something could be done, that there was an example where somebody stepped in. Hope was there.

And we rebuilt that town. It is now, it is now a fully-functioning town. Still much more work to do. But it is viable. It is a viable town there.

And we asked the rest of the world. It was $2 million. It wasn't $50 million or $200 million, it was $2 million that moved the needle from being a town that was empty to a town that was viable. And why were we able to do it for $2 million? Because there is no middleman, there is no go-between. It came to the church. The church put it right in the hands of the people. The people started rebuilding their own homes. You would be surprised at how far $2 million can go when you put it into the hands of the homeowners themselves so that they can rebuild their own towns and get out of living in IDP centers.

And, so, we have this example. And we intend to build on that with the Nineveh Reconstruction Committee. In addition to the $2 million that was initially put into Teleskov by the Hungarian Government, we have received a similar donation from the Knights of Colombus, $2 million for the town of Karamdes. And we have received another large amount from Aid to Church in Need to work on other towns in the other sectors.

It still leaves us about $22 million short of finishing all of this. But $22 million we think we can, we can make all of these towns viable so that they can be held and not taken away by other groups that want to change their demographics.

Mr. SMITH. Shireen, you, and perhaps any of you who would like to speak to this, but several years ago I authored what is known as the Torture Victims Relief Act, and it provides assistance to torture victims in these centers to people who have undergone torture at the hands of a government or an organization. And I have learned from the hearings that we had during the markups, and there were four separate laws over the course of several years, the devastating impact psychologically from torture and maltreatment at the hands of ISIS, for example.

And I am wondering what kind of help you have gotten. The physical scars are huge; the rapes, the brutality are horrific, but there is also the psychological consequences that often can be masked. And I am wondering, Shireen, have you been able to get help? And other Yazidis who have been horribly mistreated? And anyone else who would like to speak to this as well, is psychological help being provided, that may even be a hybrid of psychological and spiritual counseling, to help somebody through such a terrible memory?

Ms. SHIREEN. Thank you for the question. What we went through, and not just me, other Yazidi girls and others in captivity, was very severe. And those who escaped, who were rescued and live in the camps do not get the help they need, you know.

As I mentioned in my written statement to you on the type of the torture I faced in captivity, ISIS did an abdominal surgery on me. And I still today don't know why they did it and what it was for. And I went to doctors and still don't know why they did it.

Mr. WOLF. Mr. Chairman, we spoke to a woman who had been sold 20 times. She now lives in a little room. She cannot go back to her community. Sir, there needs to be a grant for counseling for the Yazidi women and the other women. They need something to counsel them. And it ought to be bringing counselors on the ground so they can stay in their, their community.

But they just come back. This woman is living in a little room. The Catholic Church over there is helping her. She can't go back to her community. It's a shame environment. So there needs to be something that we have been asking for a year to do something, and nothing happens.

We met with the leader of the Yazidi community Baba Shaweesh who has a little program, but it's a little, little, little, little, little program. So there needs to be a major effort. These women have been—and we had a woman come by my office, Bazi. Anybody know Bazi? The person who had her and who was abusing her was an American citizen. He was an American. He used to show her on his cell phone pictures of his wife and children back in the United States.

So we have a moral responsibility. Send over International Justice Network (IJN). Send over counselors. But there needs to be a major program. Frankly, I think this is a real test for Mark Green. When I saw Mark Green got this appointment I thought it was great. The success or failure of what takes place in Iraq for things like this may very well be on Mark Green. And if they fail, Mark Green will have failed.

So this is a major program. And people talk about it but really not very much is really being done.

Mr. GARRETT. Mr. Chairman.

Mr. KASIM. May I make a small comment? So, I am Shireen's interpreter today but I am an American citizen but I was born and raised in Iraq in Sinjar town. I worked for the U.S. military for 5 years, and that is how I came here.

Mr. SMITH. Why don't you identify yourself for the record?

Mr. KASIM. My name is Abed, Abed Kasim.

Mr. SMITH. Thank you.

Mr. KASIM. So I spent most of 2016 among IDP, like Mr. Wolf said. I mean those women, those girls who escape and survive from ISIS they have many needs. But it is hard to treat someone psychologically living in a small tent, knowing that their families are missing. They can't go back to their hometowns. They know that there are no other solutions for them. It's hard; they don't have any income.

And so it is even some of those organizations like Mr. Rasche said, I mean the help is there but it doesn't get to them. You know, they spend millions of dollars through U.N. agencies but it really doesn't get to where it needs to go.

Mr. SMITH. Mr. Garrett.

Mr. GARRETT. I queried Congressman Wolf if there is any identifying information available to the American citizen who allegedly perpetrated those acts, and if it has been forwarded to the appropriate authorities? Because I, having spent nearly 10 years as a prosecutor, can assure you that the wherewithal exists and there are means to ensure that that individual, if we can identify him and corroborate the allegations, never comes back to this country a free person.

So, if you have that information, please get it to us if it hasn't already been forwarded to the appropriate law enforcement entities.

Mr. WOLF. That is why Mr. Smith's bill, H.R. 390 is so important. It really aids to do that. I mean, there should have been FBI teams going through the tunnels now, dusting, fingerprints, everything, for our own national security, too. Because when I left this place in 2014, we funded the Bureau. The Bureau came by and told me there were 200 Americans who are over fighting for ISIS. There are a large number from other European countries.

We should know who, who they are. There is a visa waiver program so if you are from another country in Europe you can fly in. So, Mr. Smith's bill, the bill that you all did, is exactly right on target for this. That is why it ought to be passed right away because it deals with aid and assistance to Steve's group, and the other group, and Yazidis and all. But it also deals with regard to prosecution.

Mr. SMITH. And as you know, Mr. Wolf, in the past the accountability piece has been left out. And that is why believing that if we don't have people who have committed these atrocities held to account, prosecuted, it leads to impunity. And to the victims it leads to a very real—from their point of view—an existential threat to their families and communities because the bad guys are still there. We have seen a lot of that happening in Srpska and elsewhere where they did not effectively go after the people who have committed these crimes.

And the accountability piece, and thank you for underscoring it in H.R. 390, is intended to do just that. Information does fade. Facts that need to be, to be used in a prosecution are lost unless you actively, you know, retain them in a way that can be used in a prosecution.

Ms. Shireen in your written testimony you said that Abu Ali, an ISIS member who organized your kidnaping and enslavement, is living in an IDP camp near Mosul. And I am wondering if you have told any government officials from Iraq, the U.S., or elsewhere about him? And how did they respond and did they say they would do anything?

Ms. SHIREEN. Yes, that is true. I recognized him when he was being interviewed, fleeing among civilians from Tal Afar. He is the one that is responsible for selling me and many other Yazidi girls, along with another guy from Tal Afar Haji Mahdi. And I saw him, I recognized him once I saw him on T.V. And there are many like him that are just getting away with what they did to Yazidis.

Mr. SMITH. And did you convey that information to any official, U.S. or otherwise?

Ms. SHIREEN. Yes, I am hoping to speak to someone about what I know about him but I haven't yet. [Shows photos.] In these pictures my family members who are missing, some of them. And this is me when I escaped from ISIS among the other survivors.

But that guy was responsible for what happened to me and my family.

Mr. SMITH. Let me just ask, Mr. Wolf, if I could, thank you for your idea of the interagency coordinator. I think that especially in this administration where it does not have the equivalent of the NCO Corps, no head is around unless it has non-commissioned officers. The secretary, assistant secretaries and the real policy people, the nuts and bolts of the State Department and USAID are not in place. It took months for Mark Green to get in place. He has only been there for several weeks now.

So, I think the importance of an interagency coordinator, your idea, I think is absolutely compelling. And we will certainly do everything we can to push that. And I thank you for that. And you might want to elaborate on it because, again, we are on automatic pilot right now with the Obama policies.

Mr. Rasche will tell you, they have not gotten aid. I remember when I met with some of the high clerics during our visit they were grateful that finally there would be an end of the gross indifference to the Christians and the Yazidis in Erbil. And, unfortunately, it is continuing through negligence, or whatever the reason is. And it is about time. The bill would mandate it. It would finally get us to where we want to be.

And, again, you might want to make, as I have done as recently as 4 hours ago, another appeal to the Senate to bring that bill to the Floor. It is out of the Foreign Relations Committee. It has bipartisan support from the Senate side. Just put it to a vote by unanimous consent or any other means that they deem appropriate, but get it voted upon.

Then it comes back here with some tweaks. We pass it, hopefully almost immediately, it is down to the President and a gaping hole that has been an unmet need for years will finally be met.

So, if you wanted to elaborate on your coordinator idea, Mr. Wolf, because we need a point person who can get the job done. We talked about Senator Danforth. That lead to the comprehensive peace agreement. Without him there was no comprehensive peace agreement and the war between the north and the south, would have persisted, and had already claimed 2 million dead, 4 million displaced at the time. He came in and was the key to making that happen.

So your idea is extraordinary.

Mr. WOLF. Well, I think that is what you need. And personnel is policy. And if the President and Secretary Tillerson does it in the White House that will send a message to all the career people, will send a message, also, it will send a message to the Yazidi community in Iraq. It will send a message to the Christian community in Iraq. It will send a message to the world.

And, frankly, to these people that did that to her ought to be prosecuted. And we should learn from history. After the genocide the Nazis embedded in and went different places. We had to track them down. We had a Justice Department office that tracked them down. Rwanda, did the same thing. Srebenica, some of the Croats and some of the Serbs got embedded in and moved all over. We had to track them down. We should be tracking this guy down.

There should be a team going out and arresting that guy now, taking him, taking him to the International Criminal Court. If we know he is in a refugee camp, and who is paying for that refugee camp? The U.N. And who is getting the money from the U.N., who is paying the U.N., ah, the United States Government. So, maybe are you saying the United States Government is funding a camp where a man that did this to her is living?

Well, I tell you, boy, you, you need somebody really strong that could go in and sit down with the President, can sit down with Tillerson, can sit down with everybody to get this done. That is unacceptable. I didn't know that. You guys ought to be calling the FBI today and sending the FBI legal attache over there and going into that camp and taking that guy out by his collar and bringing him back to the United States or take him to the Criminal Court. My goodness, I can't believe that.

Mr. GARRETT. Mr. Chairman.

Mr. SMITH. One second before I yield to my friend.

David Crane, the former Chief Prosecutor for the Sierra Leone Special Court which put Charles Taylor, the President of Liberia, behind bars for 50 years, which is where he is now at The Hague, he is not only in favor of our bill, he has been a strong advocate and helped us, you know, in fashioning some of the language, he has made clear, right there where you sit as a witness, that without accountability a random impunity will occur and people will say, I can do whatever I want. I can rape, kill, maim, all kind of atrocities without there being a accountability in terms of a jail term.

So, again, H.R. 390 couldn't be clearer in its accountability piece. Its focus is humanitarian and on accountability. And, again, it is just waiting to be passed on the Senate side. And, hopefully, they will do it this week.

My colleague.

Mr. GARRETT. Let me say this, again, I get passionate about some things. And having been a prosecutor for about a decade I get passionate about this stuff.

This bill is important. We need to pass this bill. But I looked through U.S. Code 2330 or 2339, Subs A through D, and 2332, and I will tell you that I could put the American citizen into the prison today with the laws that are already on the books. So I would ask the subcommittee chair if it might be possible to convene a hearing, perhaps in public and perhaps in private, to assess—and because I have seen this from my work in Homeland Security as well, American citizens who travel abroad, and we have ways of knowing who they are. What is being done? Well, you know. To try to identify these individuals and bring them to justice.

At the very least, the fact that someone would flaunt their citizenship as they exploited a person who had been sold into—I won't describe in detail the type of conditions—is beyond my ability to wrap my brain around in the year 2017. And but there are apparatuses at our disposal now. We need to make it a priority. And I think this committee might take a step in that direction.

And, again, I am a co-sponsor of the bill. It's a great bill. You give me the forum in a criminal Federal court in the United States and I can, and I can take care of these guys with the laws that are already on the books. Why aren't we doing it?

And this is the second time, once in Homeland and once in this committee, where I found out about Americans allegedly cavorting with the likes of ISIS abroad where people are like, "Well, you know." Inexcusable. And it needs to a priority. If we get that individual and leadership, that liaison to the White House, it needs to be a priority.

Thank you.

Mr. SMITH. Anything else, because we do have a vote? We have about 3 minutes left before we have to be on the Floor.

Mr. Rasche.

Mr. RASCHE. If I may, Mr. Chairman, this is on topic here but it is a message to your committee from the heads of the Christian churches of the Kurdistan region. And it is a special plea in the continuing tension between Baghdad and Erbil resulting from the Kurdish referendum. They are pleading with the United States Government to exercise all options possible to make sure that this does not deteriorate any further.

There is a real, real concern that hostilities may break out. And they are pleading with the U.S. to exercise whatever authority and influence it has to make sure that this gets solved by peaceful dialog. Because if there is fighting to break out, it will happen right on top of these Christian and Yazidi communities.

I have been asked to put that, put that to you directly.

Mr. SMITH. Thank you. Well put, and we will follow up. And I deeply appreciate it.

Without objection, testimony from the Yazidi Global Organization will be made a part of the record.

And, again, I want to thank our very distinguished witnesses for your extraordinary testimony, the work that you are doing.

I had some other questions for Ms. Ashburn. One of them was why the other people in the media have not been bringing the visibility and the light to the plight of the Christians. I think it has been appalling as well. But, thankfully, you have. And I deeply, and we all deeply appreciate that.

I want to thank all of you for your testimony. Because of the vote we do have to conclude. And this hearing is adjourned.

[Whereupon, at 1:44 p.m., the subcommittee was adjourned.]

APPENDIX

SUBCOMMITTEE HEARING NOTICE
COMMITTEE ON FOREIGN AFFAIRS
U.S. HOUSE OF REPRESENTATIVES
WASHINGTON, DC 20515-6128

Subcommittee on Africa, Global Health, Global Human Rights, and International Organizations
Christopher H. Smith (R-NJ), Chairman

October 2, 2017

TO: MEMBERS OF THE COMMITTEE ON FOREIGN AFFAIRS

You are respectfully requested to attend an OPEN hearing of the Committee on Foreign Affairs, to be held by the Subcommittee Africa, Global Health, Global Human Rights, and International Organizations in Room 2172 of the Rayburn House Office Building (and available live on the Committee website at http://www.ForeignAffairs.house.gov):

DATE: Tuesday, October 3, 2017

TIME: 12:00 p.m.

SUBJECT: Iraq and Syria Genocide Emergency Relief and Accountability

WITNESSES: The Honorable Frank Wolf
                   Distinguished Senior Fellow
                   21st Century Wilberforce Initiative
                   (*Former U.S. Representative*)

                   Shireen
                   Yazidi Survivor of ISIS Enslavement

                   Mr. Stephen Rasche
                   Legal Counsel
                   Director of Internationally Displaced Persons Assistance
                   Chaldean Catholic Archdiocese of Erbil

                   Ms. Lauren Ashburn
                   Managing Editor and Anchor
                   Eternal Word Television Network

By Direction of the Chairman

COMMITTEE ON FOREIGN AFFAIRS

MINUTES OF SUBCOMMITTEE ON *Africa, Global Health, Global Human Rights, and International Organizations* HEARING

Day_____*Tuesday*_____Date_____*10/3/17*_____Room_____*2172*_____

Starting Time ____*12:01pm*____ Ending Time ____*1:43pm*____

Recesses |____| (____to ____) (____to ____) (____to ____) (____to ____) (____to ____) (____to ____)

Presiding Member(s)

Smith, Garrett

Check all of the following that apply:

Open Session ☑
Executive (closed) Session ☐
Televised ☐

Electronically Recorded (taped) ☐
Stenographic Record ☑

TITLE OF HEARING:

Iraq and Syria Genocide Emergency Relief and Accountability

SUBCOMMITTEE MEMBERS PRESENT:

Suozzi, Garrett

NON-SUBCOMMITTEE MEMBERS PRESENT: *(Mark with an * if they are not members of full committee.)*

Gabbard

HEARING WITNESSES: Same as meeting notice attached? Yes ☑ No ☐
(If "no", please list below and include title, agency, department, or organization.)

STATEMENTS FOR THE RECORD: *(List any statements submitted for the record.)*

-*Mr. Stephen Rasche: Proposal to USAID (Ninevah Reconstruction Committee USA)*
-*Mr. Stephen Rasche: Statement on Referendum Crisis (Head of Churches in Kurdistan Region)*
-*Mr. Stephen Rasche: Assessing UNDP Minority Projects*
-*Mr. Stephen Rasche: UN Completed Project for Iraqi Christians*
-*Mr. Stephen Rasche: UNDP Minority Fact Sheet (1) (2)*
-*Hon. Frank Wolf: Iraq Report-8.16.17*
-*Hon. Christopher H. Smith: Written Testimony from Yazda*

TIME SCHEDULED TO RECONVENE _________
or
TIME ADJOURNED _____________

____
Subcommittee Staff Associate

MATERIAL SUBMITTED FOR THE RECORD BY MR. STEPHEN RASCHE, LEGAL COUNSEL, DIRECTOR OF INTERNATIONALLY DISPLACED PERSONS ASSISTANCE, CHALDEAN CATHOLIC ARCHDIOCESE OF ERBIL

THE NINEVEH

SUSTAINABLE RETURN

PROGRAM

A US-Iraqi Partnership to Respond to ISIS's Campaign
of Genocide Against the People of Iraq

ABSTRACT

The NSRP seeks to accelerate the sustainable return of Iraq's persecuted Christian and other religious minorities to the ancient Nineveh Plain through the removal of war-related rubble, rehabilitation of damaged houses, and optimize regional stabilization coordination.

Nineveh Reconstruction Committee USA

THE NINEVEH SUSTAINABLE RETURN PROGRAM

AN UNSOLICITED PROPOSAL - US AGENCY FOR INTERNAITONAL DEVELOPMENT

Requesting Organization
Nineveh Reconstruction Committee USA
1314 Massachusetts Ave NW, Suite 403
Washington, DC 20005
Corporate Status: Delaware-based, 501c3 non-profit organization

Contact Persons:
Stephen Rasche
President, NRC-USA
Tel: (207) 475-2581
Email: smrasche@gmail.com

Max Primorac
Secretary/Treasurer, NRC-USA
Tel: (202) 492-7402
Email: max.primorac@yahoo.com

Project Co-funders (contact information):
Andrew T. Walther
Vice President
Communications and Strategic Planning, Knights of Columbus
One Columbus Plaza
New Haven, CT 06510
Tel: (203) 752-4253 (office)
Email: Andrew.Walther@kofc.org

Philip Ozores
Secretary General, Aid to the Church in Need International
Westerbachstrasse 23
61476, Kronberg GERMANY
Tel: (+49) 6174-291-0
Email: projects@acn-intl.org

Date of Submission: September 11, 2017

Abstract

As a consequence of ISIS' genocidal campaign against religious minorities in Iraq, these groups are experiencing the lowest rate of return among Iraqis. The Nineveh Reconstruction Committee USA seeks funding from the US Government to support its Nineveh Sustainable Return Program (NSRP). The program seeks to remove war-related rubble, rehabilitate over 9,000 partially damaged homes in seven towns, and optimize donor-funded stabilization projects in the region. To date, the $29.5 million project has received $7 million in financial support allowing for the repair of 2,254 minority homes and revival of two minority towns in the Nineveh Plain. NRC USA seeks another $22.5 million to complete this program. Absent further funding this program will end prematurely and jeopardize this community's survival.

Support from the US Government will allow us to accelerate sustainable minority returns to the Nineveh Plain. US Government support will also optimize regional donor-financed stabilization, promote inter-ethnic peace, maintain Iraq's pluralistic foundation, defeat ISIS's extremist ideology, attract larger amounts of private investment, and jump start the region's devastated economy in advance of next year's national elections. NRC-USA submits this unsolicited application for a grant or cooperative agreement in accordance with USAID's *Grants and Cooperative Agreements to non-Governmental Organizations, section 303.3.5.5 "Unsolicited Concept Papers and Applications,"* and the statutory exceptions outlined in the Office of the Procurement Executive's *Justification for Other than Full and Open Competition Guide*.

Background

On March 17, 2016 Secretary of State John Kerry pronounced ISIS "responsible for genocide" against Christians, Yezidis, and other religious minorities. On August 15, 2017 Secretary of State Rex Tillerson affirmed the official US Government policy determination that "ISIS is clearly responsible for genocide against Yezidis, Christians, and Shia Muslims in areas it controls or has controlled." The Nineveh Plain, ancient homeland of Iraq's religious minorities, was deliberately and systematically targeted by ISIS that sought to eradicate any vestige of a Christian minority presence through mass expulsion, murder, rape and the physical destruction of their religious, cultural and habitable infrastructure. This year's State Department report on international religious freedom states that since 2003 the Christian population in Iraq has declined from 1.4 million to fewer than 250,000.

As a result of this genocidal campaign, Christian settlements suffered relatively more physical damage, resulting in low rates of return to liberated lands. According to local Church and international officials, the Christian minority has seen the lowest rate of return among all Iraqi IDPs. East Mosul, for example, has seen 90% of its displaced persons return home compared to Nineveh Plain's 12% though the latter was liberated months earlier. This sectarian-based return gap reflects the unique large scale and deliberate destruction of Christian towns and represents a substantial impediment to the maintenance of a pluralistic Iraq in the future, something which is vital to the US national interest and regional security.

International donors tasked with post-ISIS stabilization have been slow to respond to the needs of these persecuted minorities who have turned to privately-funded Churches and NGOs for support. A depopulated Nineveh Plain, control over which is disputed by the central and Kurdish regional governments, threatens Iraq's stability as it encourages sectarian-based militias from other parts of Iraq to stake competing claims over these lands. Militia presence has already stoked sectarian-based clashes. The failure of this minority community to reestablish itself would represent an ideological victory for ISIS' brand of extremism and destroy Iraq's pluralistic foundation. This grave situation calls for an urgent US Government aid response.

In February 2017, the Nineveh Reconstruction Committee formed in Erbil, Iraq to plan for the return of minority IDPs to towns in the Nineveh Plain. The NRC conducted damage assessment and population intent surveys. Engineering teams catalogued the destruction of almost 13,000 private homes and damage to schools, health clinics, public and religious and cultural buildings (survey data can be obtained at www.nrciraq.org). NRC USA identified 9,075 damaged homes fit for rehabilitation or removal at a cost of $29.5 million. These findings constitute the baseline data for the Nineveh Sustainable Return Program. Since February, the NSRP has received $7 million in financial support from Europe-based Aid to the Church in Need International, US-based Knights of Columbus, and the Government of Hungary. This support is resulting in the rehabilitation of 2,254 homes and organized return of several thousand IDPs, restoring community life to two previously depopulated towns and providing initial footholds in others. Another $22.5 million is needed to complete the program. NRC USA's coalition of local Churches, NGOs, construction and other businesses is uniquely positioned to partner with the US Government. Absent additional funding assistance this program will terminate prematurely and jeopardize this community's survival.

Objectives

- Accelerate sustainable returns of Iraq's persecuted minorities to multi-confessional areas of northern Iraq, politically stabilize the volatile Nineveh Plain, and optimize donor-funded humanitarian and stabilization programs in Ninawa Province.

- Support the legitimacy of the Government of Iraq, strengthen provincial and local government, ensure long-term peace among Iraq's peoples, sustain Iraq's pluralistic foundation, and prevent the resurgence of ISIS's ideology of intolerance and violence.

- Set a firm community-based foundation for successful post-ISIS stabilization and larger-scale reconstruction, political reconciliation, and inclusive participation in next year's national elections for parliament and provincial government.

Methodology

Stabilization Capacities Forged by Humanitarian Disaster Response

The NRC USA's methodology draws from its experience providing life-saving disaster relief for up to130,000 Christians IDPs since 2014. Led by the Chaldean Catholic Archdiocese of Erbil in coordination with local notables, civic groups, businesses, and local officials, various types of temporary housing facilities, including large-scale camps, were established in multiple locations where IDPs from a variety of religious minority communities, but also non-minority IDPs, have been provided shelter, water, food, sanitation, basic health, primary and secondary education, cash grants, winterization kits, and other critical supplies and services. These relief activities have been supported by Aid to the Church in Need (ACN) International, a Europe-based pontifical foundation, and Knights of Columbus, a US-based charitable organization, along with dozens of other private charitable organizations worldwide, totaling over $40 million in direct financial support fully managed and implemented by the Archdiocese and its local affiliates. It is from this tested local project management and civic infrastructure of Churches, NGOs, businesses and experts that the Nineveh Reconstruction Committee was formed in February 2017 in order to facilitate transition from humanitarian relief to resettlement and stabilization operations in newly liberated areas of Ninawa Province. Today, about 95,000 IDPs still rely on relief support but anxiously await an opportunity to return home to the Nineveh Plain.

Community Empowerment for Sustainable Returns

Based on a survey of population intent within the IDP and nearby refugee communities, we have determined that a majority of them would like to return home but that residential destruction and lack of external financing to repair their dwellings were decisive factors blocking their return home. A February 2017 survey found that 41% of respondents wanted to return home, up from about 3% six months earlier, demonstrating the profound impact that hope of external material support can have on people's intent to rebuild their former lives. Today, we estimate that at least 65% of IDPs will return home in the Nineveh Plain if their dwellings are made habitable.

A damage assessment survey[1] conducted by a team of local engineers, architects, and financial and project management experts, catalogued 12,419 houses in the Nineveh Plain that were either damaged, burned or destroyed. Based on this survey and estimated costs to repair those dwellings, we identified 8,078 homes that can be rapidly rehabilitated for resettlement, and an additional 997 destroyed homes which must be cleared and removed so that safe restoration and stabilization of the communities can begin. An implementation plan was drawn up. Initial funding from ACN International, Knights of Columbus, and the Government of Hungary totaling $5 million, with another $2 million secured from other smaller donors, allowed the NRC coalition to initiate the first set of home restorations. With these initial funds, in the past two months, 2,254 homes have been or are being repaired in two previously devastated communities. Site selection, costing of construction materials, and financial and program management is being executed by a team of local architects, engineers, and construction firms on the ground with decades of commercial experience in the private construction and public infrastructure sectors.

---

[1] The survey was conducted in Al Qosh, Teleskuf, Baqofa, Batnaya, Telkef, Bazhani, Bashiqa, Bartella, Karamles, and Qaraqosh.

Nearly 100% of all program spending, including procurement of construction materials, is conducted through local businesses, construction companies, professional experts and labor. This approach maximizes the impact of donor funding on reviving the local economy and generating local employment, both necessary to sustainable resettlement and, with it, long term economic development and political reconciliation. Such a program implementation approach deters permanent population departures and emigration of professional and educated workers that are critical to the long term economic and political stabilization of the region.

With US Government funding, NRC USA will be able to continue and expand its on-going sustainable return program and complete it in time for Iraq's national elections set for late 2018. Absent additional funding this program will end prematurely and jeopardize this community's survival. Below are the key program components of the Nineveh Sustainable Return Program:

Program Component #1: *Rubble Removal*

Those homes, public and commercial buildings, and infrastructure that are destroyed beyond repair along with other war-related debris must be removed for environmental, safety, and confidence-building reasons. These hazardous areas represent significant risk to life and limb, especially for children, and must be immediately removed in order to ensure sustainable IDP returns to this area. With the appropriate equipment, this phase can be initiated immediately and completed prior to the onset of winter. Rubble removal will also accelerate the execution of stabilization projects planned by other donor-funded initiatives. The following seven settlements have been selected for rubble removal: Batnaya, Bahzani, Bashiqa, Bartulla, Karamles, Qaraqosh, and Teleskof. We have identified local construction equipment operators, equipment maintenance workers, and general physical labor that we can immediately deploy to launch this phase of the project. Employment of local people will help regenerate local economies and attract a larger amount of private capital for longer-term economic development of this region. The equipment we require is listed below and will be utilized strictly and only in support of this program. NRC USA will coordinate closely with local Iraqi security and other government authorities with respect to ensuring that areas designated for rubble and debris removal are cleared of mines and unexploded ordinance. The US Government has funded major demining programs in the Nineveh Province and the NSRP builds on that investment.

With US Government support, the NRC will purchase or lease the following rubble-removal equipment listed below from local suppliers that currently have supplied US Department of Defense contractors supporting Coalition efforts to defeat ISIS. NRC USA has identified available and qualified machine operators and mechanics who have been trained on maintaining this equipment and on how to adhere properly to all safety and environmental laws, regulations and guidelines of the Government of Iraq as well as to international donor standards.

- Wheel loaders (2)
- Rigid dump trucks (2)
- Skid steer loaders (2)

Program Component #2: *Rehabilitation of Damaged Homes*

These communities have suffered substantial physical damage from ISIS and coalition military strikes to expel the terrorists from these lands. Worse, these towns have yet to see the restoration of water and power as the UNDP lags in executing stabilization projects in the Nineveh Plain. In order to ensure immediate and sustainable returns, the NRC USA will (1) initiate the repair of thousands of homes while (2) coordinating with donors supporting stabilization projects to restore water, power, and other critical basic public services in areas of minority returns. The NRC USA will tap into its roster of infrastructure, and construction engineers, architects, accountants, general contractors, and labor to rehabilitate residential dwellings and execute basic infrastructure works. The NRC USA will apply the program and financial management capability developed from its on-going humanitarian aid work and initiation of the Nineveh Sustainable Return Program, totaling over $40 million in funding to date.

Seven towns have been identified for this rehabilitation program (Batnaya, Bahzani, Bashiqa, Bartulla, Karamles, Qaraqosh, Teleskof) and in each town individual dwellings have been identified as fit for rehabilitation as assessed through a survey conducted by our team of engineers and architects. Our surveys indicate that 35% of the displaced population may well not return to their homes in the Nineveh Plain. We have excluded from the rehabilitation project list all dwellings whose owners have been registered as non-returnees. Each dwelling will be restored to habitability and the return of owners carefully coordinated, monitored, and evaluated post-rehabilitation. Survey data has been digitally catalogued. The monitoring and evaluation process will occur simultaneously with the actual rehabilitation and the lessons drawn from the evaluation will be fed back into our program implementation plan in order to improve program effectiveness. Project materials and work requirements have been previously determined by our team of construction engineers and architects with support from other local businesses in order to accelerate the rehabilitation timeline. See the section on Project Cost for additional information.

Table 1: Summary of Estimates for Rehabilitation of Dwellings

	Destroyed/ID for removal	Burned/ID for Repair	Damaged/ID for Repair	Under Repair
Batnaya	521	69	222	34
Bahzani	60	45	117	
Bashiqa	50	127	218	
Bartulla	94	226	892	
Karamles	89	241	424	600
Qaraqosh	115	1,568	2,730	720
Teleskof	69	95	1,104	900
Total Houses ID	997	2,371	5,707	2,254
Est Cost per House (USD)	1,500	7,000	2,000	3,000
Est Total Cost (USD)	1,495,500	16,597,000	11,414,000	6,762,000
TOTAL HOUSES ID FOR REPAIR/REMOVAL	9.075			
TOTAL PROJECT COST (USG)	29,506,500			
TOTAL HOUSES PRESENTLY UNDER REPAIR	2,254			
TOTAL FUNDS PRESENTLY ALLOCATED	7,000,000			
TOTAL FUNDING REQUEST	22,506,500			
TOTAL HOUSES FOR FUNDING REQUEST	6,821			

US Government funding will build on the program's achievements to date: Through $7 million in grants from ACN International, Knights of Columbus, the Government of Hungary, and other donors, the NRC USA coalition recently rehabilitated or is rehabilitating 2,254 homes in Teleskof and Karamles, with foothold operations ongoing in other communities.

Program Component #3: *Coordinating Restoration of Water, Power, and other Public Services*

The United Nations Development Programme leads post-ISIS stabilization efforts in the four ISIS-affected provinces. Its Fund Facility for Stabilization has planned and executed a number of projects to rehabilitate local infrastructure to facilitate sustainable returns and succeeded in facilitating the return of millions of IDPs. Its record of achievement in minority areas, however, has been poor. Despite initiating over 1,000 stabilization projects, UNDP has completed only two of them in the Nineveh Plain, reflecting the lack of local community participation in project prioritization, coordination and execution.

Through US Government support, NRC USA will strengthen its local partners' institutional capacity to more effectively coordinate with the UNDP, the Government of Iraq, other donor officials, and donor-implementing partners and integrate our rehabilitation project with the restoration of critical public services, such as water, sewerage, power, health, and school services. NRC USA will also help its local partners to coordinate more closely and effectively with multi-donor Cluster Coordination Committees for WASH, logistics, food security, health, camps and other sectors.

We have engaged Dr. Mostafa Al Hiti, Head of the central government's Iraq's Reconstruction Fund, to coordinate our rehabilitation activities with his national government reconstruction and infrastructure plans, including as a feeder of engineering data on damaged local and provincial level infrastructure. Dr. Al Hiti shares NRC USA's view that targeted and coordinated donor and Iraqi government stabilization and infrastructure support must be conducted in a manner that attracts a far larger amount of local, national, and international private capital. NRC USA has already received preliminary interest from major wealth centers to invest in local private sector industries valued in the tens of millions of dollars and will pursue this private sector development opportunity through other resources.

Expected Results

Through the Nineveh Sustainable Return Program, the NRC USA expects that minority returns to the Nineveh Plain region will approximate those percentages reached in other parts of Iraq, specifically the ISIS-effected provinces.

Note: The previous material submitted for the record is not reprinted here in its entirety but may be accessed in full on the Internet at the following address: http://docs.house.gov/Committee/Calendar/ByEvent.aspx?EventID=106459

Statement of the Heads of the Christian Churches in the Kurdistan Region on the Referendum Crisis

Blessed are the peacemakers, for they will be called children of God.

(Mathew 9:5)

STATEMENT

In the aftermath of the last regime change, the Iraqi Christians have been exposed to a continued series of painful attacks. These began with the attacks by Al-Qaida, through those of the Islamic party militias, to gangs belonging to organized crime, and ending with the gangs of ISIS, which forcefully displaced our people from Mosul and the Plain of Nineveh. During this time the successive governments that came to power after 2003 failed to defend and safeguard the Christian component of the Iraqi citizens, and failed to protect their legal rights.

This has led to the emigration of many Iraqi Christians. At present, our future does not appear to hold any good for us, nor does it indicate a continuation of Christian existence in this part of the world where Christianity has existed since the first century AD.

Amidst these attacks and the prevailing situation, wherein one crises breeds another, the Christians along with other components of the Iraqi people are the ones who pay the price of religious, sectarian, and political struggles that have weighed heavily on them: killing them, setting them astray, taking their lives and possessions, and bombing and setting on fire their churches and lands.

It is possible to say without any doubt that it is the Christians who continue to be the biggest losers in all of these fights, to which they have never been party and which, if continued, would render our people more intent on emigration, leading to their being wiped out from the surface of this land.

Undoubtedly, we Christians can never forget how our brothers in Kurdistan Region, as a people and government, received us and supported our displaced persons, not only Christians but also other components of the Iraqi people. The Kurdistan Region was a safe haven for us during the successive plights that have befallen us since 2003. As such, we are very concerned that this region now remains safe for those who live in it.

We appeal to the conscience of humanity, the international community, the UN and the major powers to intervene and bear their moral and human responsibility to safeguard our people and help them stay and survive on their ancestral land through the following efforts:

1. The creation of conditions for dialogue based on mutual respect between the Iraqi Federal Government and the Kurdistan Regional Government on the disputed issues, and a move away from the language of threats and the use of media for escalating the crisis. In this there must be an aim to reach a suitable solution apart from spreading the feelings of hatred that fuel conflicts. It is a clear fact that this situation has created in Christians a state of fear and concern about the possibility that the struggle may develop into a crisis that will have far reaching repercussions for all.

2. Keeping Christians safe from the internal struggles among the larger components of the Iraqi people. We cannot hide our concern that the situation for the Christians has become very difficult and leads to uncertainty. Amidst the absence of any genuine political plans for them, the Christians are unable to see the path that would help them stay and survive on their ancestral land in dignity. Our people are tired of more injury, disappointment and frustration. Our communities are unable to withstand further the emigration of those of our people who still remain.

3. Restoration of life to the Christian towns and their reconstruction, and the development of projects that would provide job opportunities for their children so that their existence may continue in the area. While both the federal government and the KRG are engaged in struggle over the disputed area, including the historical areas of our people, the areas liberated from the control of the criminal ISIS gangs are in an appalling condition in terms of reconstruction, public services, and security. There are no serious attempts at reconstructing the area at all by the governments. This makes it difficult for the IDPs to return, thereby prolonging their plight.

4. Termination of all acts of demographic change in the Christian historical areas that would bring about change to its Christian identity. Care should be taken not use vulnerable Christians and arm them to serve agendas that do not serve the genuine interests of our Christian people. We demand that the use of arms be restricted to the official government security forces, which we encourage our young men to join.

5. The future Plain of Nineveh should be maintained as a unified territory; it is critical to not divide it into parts. Care should be made not to involve the last remaining Christian land in political bargaining, as our vulnerable community cannot withstand further schism and division in addition to the ongoing political and sectarian fights. The Plain of Nineveh is a great symbol for Christians in Iraq, the Kurdistan Region, and the world.

Amidst the crisis that the country experiences today following the referendum of Kurdistan Region, we call upon all parties involved to opt for dialogue and moderation and to stop the escalation of the conflict through the media. We call upon them all to make efforts to contain the internal crises between the conflicting politicians through serious dialogue based on the recognition of the other and respecting their rights. Efforts should also be made to overcome all the challenges in a way that makes all as equal partners in preparing secure living conditions, especially when everybody is weary of the ongoing crises and their ramifications, especially the Christians who must not be used any further as fuel for more wars and crises.

We stress that there is no other means to solve the problems of the country other than to seriously and genuinely sit at the table of negotiation for dialogue so that everyone may have their rights. We do not encourage the internationalization of these conflicts and the intervention of others, as the latter will only further complicate things and make the people of Iraq, with all of its ethnic and religious components, destined to further endless conflicts.

We pray to God to lead all to the right path, the path of peace, justice, charity and dignity.

Heads of the Christian Churches in the Kurdistan Region

Archbishop BASHAR WARDA
Archbishop NEQODEMOUS DAWOUD SHARIF
Archbishop APRIS JOUNSEN
Bishop Rabban AL QAS
Archbishop MOUSA AL SHAMANE

Sunday, 1 October 2017

55

Assessing UNDP's Project List to Support Minority Returns to Nineveh Plain

Local aid delivery leaders from Iraq's Christian minority complain that US and UN aid agencies bypass their community when allocating humanitarian and stabilization funds. The State Department, however, points to a July, 2017 UN report claiming there are 152 projects underway in eight Christian districts in their homeland of Nineveh Plain, valued at $34 million. US and UN officials cannot verify completion of these projects due to travel restrictions. Neither are Christian leaders consulted on project selection. We reviewed the veracity of the attached project list based on on-site information provided by local aid leaders operating in those districts. We conclude that the UN report grossly exaggerates its support of Iraq's Christian minority returns.

1. The report includes Telkayf which was entirely cleansed of Christians by ISIS fighters colluding with local Sunni residents. ISIS fighters were expelled but their local collaborators remain and Iraqi authorities have relocated captured ISIS families there. Christian are terrified to return home. In effect, UNDP projects are rewarding ethno-religious cleansing.

2. Districts Hamm Al-Alil and Nimrud, or 2 of the 8 districts, are non-Christian.

3. The major Christian town of Telskof is excluded, while two other important Christian settlements (Baqof, Bartella) see the smallest number of project activities among these districts.

4. While UNDP cites power and water as priorities, Christian districts do not have power and water.

5. Hamdaniyah has the largest number of Christian residents but it is a very mixed district. Most projects cited are mostly cosmetic - paint overs, cleaning, but not basic infrastructure, like water and power.

6. Local NGOs cannot confirm completion of many cited projects, indicating they may be paper completions in which money is spent but projects are not completed, similar to how pre-ISIS Iraqi government contracting funds were pilfered. Local NGOs say UN contracts must include a 7% mark up to cover illicit payments to UN officials. As US Embassy and UN officials cannot eye these programs themselves they rely on reports by UN administrators and their Iraqi contractors.

7. Completion of the As Salamiyah Water Treatment is often cited as a major project benefitting 100,000 people in Nineveh Plain. Local engineers say the plant is physically located in Nineveh Plain but the 100,000 served are mostly non-Christians near Mosul. It is seen as a good project but not one for Christians.

8. The UNDP last quarterly report claims "The majority of those displaced from the [Nineveh Plain] have not yet returned home, and have demonstrated a reluctance to return without guarantees of their security and the stability of their towns and villages." UNDP fails to mention that their homes are inhabitable. Church surveys show nearly two-thirds want to retur if their homes are repaired. The Nineveh Reconstruction Committee, a joint project of the three main Churches there, have repaired over 2,000 homes in Telskof and Karamles recently and Christians returned home.

Outsourcing US aid programs to the UN is not working for Iraq's victimized Christian minority. Church-based organizations, in contrast, have proved highly effective in implementing successful projects at lower cost, minus corruption, through local engagement, generate local employment and economic development, with on-site monitoring. USAID should change its aid delivery approach and work through tested local Church and aid organizations.

END

"Atrocities in Iraq and Syria: Relief for Survivors and Accountability for Perpetrators"
House Foreign Committee, Subcommittee on Africa, Global Health, Global Human Rights, and International Organizations

Testimony by Stephen M. Rasche, Esq
Legal Counsel & Director of IDP Resettlement Programs,
Chaldean Catholic Archdiocese of Erbil, Kurdistan, Iraq
Tuesday, October 3, 2017

Sample: UN "Completed Project" to Support Christian Returns – a school project in Teleskof

- School Courtyard Exterior – (UN logo)

UN Refurbished School in Teleskof

- **Teleskof School Classroom Building Interior (no UN logo)**

UN Refurbished School in Teleskof

- **School classroom – Exterior (UN logo)**

UN Refurbished School in Teleskof

- **School Interior yard – for recess playtime (no UN logo)**

FUNDING FACILITY FOR STABILIZATION

July 2017

2,000,000
displaced Iraqis have returned home since January 2014

1,100
stabilization projects have been completed or are underway in 23 locations in Iraq

152
projects support mainly Christian communities in the Ninewa Plains, valued at USD 34 million

100,000
people in the Ninewa Plains have access to safe water after the rehabilitation of the As-Salamiyah Water Treatment Plant

70
projects support Yazidi communities in Snga, Sinuni and Rabia, valued at USD 23 million

- At the request of the Iraqi Prime Minister, the Funding Facility for Stabilization (FFS) was established in June 2015 to help the Government rehabilitate public infrastructure in the areas newly liberated from ISIL as quickly as possible and facilitate the return of people displaced from their homes.

- The approach is pragmatic and swift. Within days of a city being declared safe, stabilization teams conduct damage assessments and agree on urgent needs with local authorities. Priority is given to: repairing essential public infrastructure including water systems and electricity grids; employing youth on work brigades to remove rubble, open transport routes and revitalize the city; providing cash grants to businesses to reopen; and rehabilitating schools, health centres, and administrative buildings.

- The Facility is currently implementing more than 1,000 projects in 22 locations. The impact is significant. Last year, more than one million Iraqis returned to newly liberated areas; the Facility channeled USD 93 million into these areas.

FLAGSHIP PROGRAMME FOR MINORITY COMMUNITIES

- In November 2016, a special window was opened to support minority communities in newly liberated areas and help give Chaldean and Assyrian Christians, Shabak and Yazidis confidence in their future in Iraq.

- Using fast track procedures, the Facility is implementing 70 projects in northern Ninewa and more than 150 projects in the Ninewa Plains. Tens of infrastructure projects have already been completed in Sinuni and Rabea and stabilization work is accelerating in Nimrud, Hamdaniyah, Karamless, Bartela, Bashiqa, Telkayf, Telesqof, Batnaya, Al-Qosh, and Sheikhan.

- At the request of communities, infrastructure and employment are being prioritized. The water treatment plant has been rehabilitated in Nimrud and the main transmission line between Hamdaniyah and As-Salamiyah is now operational. The hospital and eight primary health centers in Hamdaniyah are being reconstructed and water, electricity and sewage infrastructure is being rehabilitated in Bashiqa, Bartela, Hamdaniyah, Telesqof and Telkayf. Throughout newly liberated areas, thousands of people are working on public schemes, earning income to support their families.

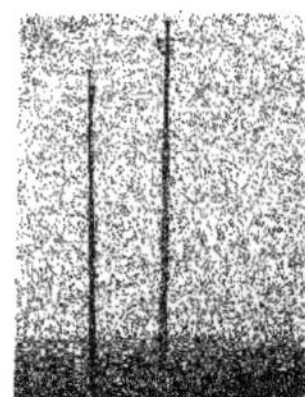

No.	Description	No.	Description	No.	Description
SINUNI		**BAQOF**		135	Education Directorate Warehouse
1	Baihalif wells and pump station	71	Water substation	136	Sanharib Industrial High School
2	Sherfadan wells	72	Primary School for Boys	137	Ur School
3	Sinuni High School	73	Primary School for Girls	138	Health Department
4	Beirut High School	**BARTELA**		139	Hamdaniyah PHC
5	Qurtuba 2 Primary School	74	Bartela PHC	140	Al Mufaqiya PHC
6	Iraq 2 Secondary School	75	Mayor Building	141	Hasan Sham PHC
7	Beirut 1 Primary School	76	Municipal workshop canopy	142	Bashdida PHC
8	Anduls Secondary School	**BASHIQA**		143	Ali Rash PHC
9	Al Tamom 4 Primary School	77	9 water wells	144	Karamless PHC
10	Al Moi School	78	Water Resources Dpt.	145	Manarah Al Shabak PHC
11	Hiten Secondary School	79	Water Office furniture	146	Medical equipment for 8 PHCs
12	Rabia Mixed School	80	Water network equipment	147	Furniture for 8 PHCs
13	Al Moi School furniture	81	Water network	148	Police Directorate
14	Hiten Secondary School furniture	82	Bashiqa PHC	149	Cash for work restoring municipal parks
15	Sinuni PHC	83	Bozaqaya PHC	150	Almaqiyat shops
16	Sinuni PHC medical equipment	84	PHC medical equipment	151	Additional shops
17	Medical equipment	85	PHC furniture	152	Karmless Municipality building
18	2 PHCs in Quhora collective towns	86	Sewage Directorate equipment and trucks	153	Street paving
19	2 PHCs in Zurava collective towns	87	Sewage Directorate work tools and labour	154	Cash for work restoring municipal parks 2
20	3 water browsers	88	Sewage Directorate	155	Hamdaniyah Power Station
21	Municipal equipment	89	Sewage network	156	Hamdaniyah Hospital Phase 1
22	Asset replacement for vulnerable women	90	Mayoral Building	157	Hamdaniyah Hospital Phase 2
23	Cash for work rubble clearance	91	Council Building	158	Hamdaniyah Hospital - medical equipment
24	3 mobile generators	92	Garbage dump	159-179	Furniture for 20 Hamdaniyah schools
25	132KV transmission line Sinuni to Al-	93	Municipal parks	**NIMRUD**	
26	Transport for 132KV line	94	Municipal shops	180	Akheba School
27	Warehouse for 132KV line materials	95	Municipality Directorate equipment	181	Al Shahed Sobhea School
28	45MVA 132/33 KV mobile sub-station	96	Municipality Warehouse	182	Al Shahed Abd Al Hamed School
29	Monitoring office	97	Agriculture Department Building	183	Al Yaeor School for Boys
SINJAR		98	Sheikhan Court generator roof	184	Said Hamad High School
30	Rolhalat wells	99	Cash for work sewage network clean-up	185	Said Hamad High School
31	Sinjar Educational Directorate	100	Substation 33/11 KV	186	Said Hamad School
32	Sinjar PHC	101	Electrical network	187	Snedee School
33	Sinjar PHC medical equipment	102	2x mobile substations	188	Tal Akob School for Boys
34	Sinjar PHC furniture	103	Electricity Directorate	189	Tal Akob School for Girls
35	Sinjar PHC additional equipment	104	Overhead 33 KV network	190	Al Abbas School
36	Municipal equipment	105	33/11 KV substation spare parts	191	Al Adlah School
37	Livelihoods support	**BATNAYA**		192	Al Nayfa School
38	2 mobile generators	106	Pump station	193	Al Nayfa School
39	132KV line Mosul Dam to Cement Factory	107	Street paving	194	Al Nomania School
40	Cement Factory Substation	**HAMAM AL-ALIL**		195	Al Salamiya School for Boys
41	33 KV line Cement Factory Substation to	108	Water project	196	Al Salamiya School for Boys
42	Repair/replace water networks	109	Al-Salamiyah Water Treatment Plant	197	Al Salamiya School for Girls
43	Cash for work rubble clearance	110	Hamam Al-Alil PHC	198	Al Tawleaiya School
RABIA		111	Municipal garage fence	199	Al Thibyania School
44	Rabia Water Directorate	112	Cash for work park construction	**TELKAYF**	
45	Rabia Education warehouse	113	132KV transmission line to Hamdaniya	200	Clean 160,000 m3 settling tanks
46	Rabia High School	**HAMDANIYAH**		201	Telkayf pump station
47	Rabia Intermediate School	114	Mar Qaragosh shops	202	Telkayf pump station
48	Abo Hmera School	115	Vegetable market	203	Telsqof pump station
49	Al Barona School	116	Road paving	204	Al Sadn School
50	Al Barnoo School	117	Water pump stations	205	Baaqtah School
51	Al gha Al Aarya School	118	Qaragosh Girls Secondary School	206	Alsada 1 School
52	Kran School	119	Qaragosh Boys Secondary School	207	Baaqtiha High School
53	Mshirfa School	120	Rasen Primary School	208	Telkayf 3 School for Boys
54	Tal Talab School	121	Al-Zawra Primary School	209	Telkayf 2 School for Boys
55	Abo Hmera School furniture	122	Qaragosh Kindergarten	210	Telkayf 2 School for Girls
56	Al Barona School furniture	123	Altaqlobia School	211	Telkayf Kindergarten
57	Rabia Mixed School furniture	124	Ashur Banibal Alrayania School	212	Telkayf PHC
58	Al Barnoo School furniture	125	Al Moalem School	213	Al Qosh PHC
59	Rabia High School furniture	126	Almutamayizin School	214	Aski Mosul PHC
60	Municipality building	127	Alkafidian School	215	Street paving
61	Municipal equipment	128	Ashor Panpoal School	216	Telsqof Mayoral Building
62	Municipal Council Building	129	Bagdeda Intermediate School	217	Municipality workshop
63	Court House	130	Ashur High School	218	Cash for work street maintenance
64	City Hall	131	Qaragosh 2 Kindergarten	219	Cash for work Telsqof street maintenance
65	Al Jazeera agricultural irrigation	132	Margam Al Adfraa High School	220	Telsqof electrical substations
66	Livelihood support vulnerable households	133	Naid Primary School	221	Telsqof 33/11 transformer station
67	Rabia substation 33 & 11 KV breakers	134	Qaragosh High School	222	Water treatment plant controller room
68	Warehouse for 132KV line materials				
69	Transfer 132KV materials MOE				
70	Internal electrical network				

Northern Iraq 2017

Congressman Frank R. Wolf (Ret. 1981-2014)
Distinguished Senior Fellow, 21st Century Wilberforce Initiative

August 16, 2017

Introduction

I. Executive Summary

The following are my personal observations and recommendations from
my recent trip to Iraq. In the summer of 2014, the world watched as
the Islamic State of Iraq and Syria began their murderous march across
much of northern Iraq, leaving in their wake a path of unimaginable
destruction. In March of 2016, the United States Congress unanimously
passed a resolution identifying the acts of ISIS against Christians,
Yazidis and other ethnic and religious minorities as genocide, crimes
against humanity and war crimes. Just a few days after the Congress
passed the resolution, Secretary of State John Kerry made an official
statement recognizing the events as genocide. However, three years on
and following the liberation of most of the Christian and Yazidi villages
in northern Iraq, including Mosul, there is an ever-increasing concern
that many of the ethnic and religious minority communities will be
unable to return homes due to the destruction, and the growing political
tensions between the central government of Iraq, the Kurdistan Regional
Government and other non-state actors. If something bold is not done
by the United States and the international community, I believe we will
see the end of Christianity in the cradle of Christendom and a loss of
religious and ethnic diversity throughout the region which could result in
further destabilization across the Middle East and present a threat to U.S.
national security interests.

Church in Qaraqosh

I have visited Iraq five times now. This August I travelled with a
delegation including Christian Solidarity Worldwide and others in order
to better understand the current situation the Christians and Yazidis
face. We went into war-torn areas where US embassy personnel are not
allowed to go because of understandable security concerns, including
Sinjar Mountain, Sinjar City, Bartella, Qaraqosh, Nimrud, Erbil, Duhok
and Mosul, which was most recently liberated from ISIS in July 2017.
In addition, we met with representatives from the central government
of Iraq, the Kurdistan Regional Government, local NGO's such as the
Assyrian Aid Society and Humanitarian Nineveh Relief Organization,
international NGO's such as Samaritan's Purse and UN agencies such
as UNICEF, International Organization for Migration (IOM), and the
UNDP, as well as Christian and Yazidi religious and political leaders. We
also visited IDP camps where we heard heartbreaking stories from men,

405 North Washington Street
Suite 300
Falls Church, Virginia 22046
www.21wilberforce.org
info@21wilberforce.org
571.297.3177

Northern Iraq Report | August 16, 2017

The Christians

women and children who had been tortured, raped, and displaced by the Islamic State.

II. The Christians

In 2003, the Christians in Iraq numbered 1.5 million. Today, that number has decreased to what most estimate is 250,000, although some argue the number is down to 150,000. I believe the number is between 200,000-300,000. Unknown too many, after Israel, Iraq is the location of more biblical history than any other country. The great patriarch Abraham came from Ur in southern Iraq, modern Nasiriyah and Rebekah came from northwest Iraq. Additionally, Jacob's sons, the 12 tribes of Israel, were all born in Iraq and Daniel lived in Iraq most of his life. Despite this, the Christian community in Iraq has been largely forgotten by many in the West.

While on the trip we spoke with several internally displaced Christian families. One family, living in a camp outside of Duhok, had fled from Bartella. When asked if they would return home the father indicated that he would since Christians are people of peace and would be willing to forgive those who wronged them. His wife, however, said, "I want to leave. Australia...anywhere in the West. For the sake of my children." She then went on to explain that she was so concerned for the well-being and safety of her 15-year-old daughter that she had kept her out of school since the family's displacement.

Another gentleman from Mosul was studying for his PhD when ISIS came and forced him to flee with his family. When asked if he would return to Mosul he said he would like to but does not believe he can since many of his neighbors indirectly considered him and his family infidels even before ISIS came. He stated, "We have no guarantees. Everyone is using us - we are caught in the middle. We asked for peace, but we cannot live with the discrimination."

One of the most heartbreaking personal accounts was the story of a Christian woman named Maryam,* who was sold as a sex slave over 20 different times, raped hundreds of times, beaten and abused. At one point while trying to escape she jumped out of a third story window and broke

Remnants of an ISIS banner in Bartella (Christian town)

Meeting an Arab family living in a church in Mosul

21ST CENTURY WILBERFORCE INITIATIVE SPEAK FREEDOM

405 North Washington Street
Suite 300
Falls Church, Virginia 22046
www.21wilberforce.org
info@21wilberforce.org
571 297 3177

The Christians

her leg. When her captor realized what had happened he beat her and left her lying on the ground. When she was eventually rescued she thought her family would welcome her back, instead a deeply entrenched honor culture compelled her family and community to reject her. Now she is afraid to walk on the street in her own community.

In addition, we met with a young boy who lived with his disabled mother. When ISIS came he tried to hide in his house, but eventually they ran out of food and ISIS fighters found them. The fighters said they must convert or die. The mother told her son they should just pretend to convert in order to survive, even though in their hearts they knew the truth. They did and ISIS allowed them to stay. However, they forced the young boy, aged 14, to join ISIS. Eventually he managed to escape with his mother. However, today they are unable to return to their hometown because no one will trust them.

Even though their homes were destroyed or looted and their lives nearly destroyed, many of the Christian families believe this can be overcome. However, the Christian communities are skeptical of security guarantees in post-ISIS Iraq. Currently, they must rely heavily on the central Iraqi government and the KRG for their protection but they lack trust in both groups since both the Arabs and Kurds have marginalized the Christian communities before.

Moreover, the tension between the Peshmerga and Iraqi Forces, including the Hashd al Shabbi, has created contested territories all throughout the Nineveh Plains, where most Christians reside. According to a top UN official, the Christians are being instrumentalized by both sides trying to claim land after ISIS. Along with the destruction of the homes and livelihood of thousands of Christians, ISIS attempted to completely destroy any memory of Christianity in Iraq by destroying ancient biblical sites and symbols, including the cross. The Assyrian Aid Society, a local Christian NGO, took me to several historical Assyrian biblical sites, including the ancient town of Nimrud, mentioned in Genesis 10. In 2015, ISIS packed the ruins of Nimrud with explosives and then filmed its detonation. Very little remains intact. When visiting churches in Mosul, Bartella and Qaraqosh, every single cross was broken, even those that

Remnants of Ancient Nimrud which ISIS blew up in 2015

405 North Washington Street
Suite 300
Falls Church, Virginia 22046
www.21wilberforce.org
info@21wilberforce.org
571 297 3177

Northern Iraq Report | August 16, 2017

The Christians/ Yazidis

had been carved into stone.

However, there are reasons to be hopeful. While estimates vary, to-date approximately 600 families have returned to their homes in the Nineveh plains. This reveals a desire within the communities to return to their ancestral homelands. In addition, NGOs and the Catholic Church are beginning house repair and rebuilding programs in the areas to assist Christians who want to rebuild their lives. However, there is much more to be done. More funding, demining and protection is essential to fully rebuild the region from ISIS's destruction.

Destruction in Sinjar

If nothing is done, I believe that we will see the end of ancient Christianity in Iraq within a few years. Currently, the population is getting dangerously close to dipping below the critical mass needed for these Christians to maintain their long-term presence in their ancestral homeland. If this trend is allowed to continue, the Christian population will follow that of the Jewish population, which has decreased from 150,000 individuals in 1948 to just 10 people today. To counteract this trend, bold action is required on the part of the United States and the West.

III. The Yazidis

The Yazidis are an ancient ethnic and religious group numbering 1 million worldwide with 600,000 living in Iraq. Sinjar is the ancient homeland of the Yazidis as well as the location of their devastating mass murder committed by the Islamic State, which began on August 3rd, 2014. Mass graves continue to be found throughout the city, one of which I saw during my visit. Along with the utter destruction of their homeland, the murder, rape and displacement of thousands of their people, over 3,000 of their women and girls are still being held by ISIS.

The images of the Yazidis fleeing Sinjar City from ISIS are still imprinted on the minds of many. However, a year and a half since the liberation of Sinjar City no more than a handful of families have returned. This is due to, not only the immense destruction, but also the unpredictable security situation the various militias on the ground have created. One of the only signs of life were the soldiers belonging to the militias controlling

21ST CENTURY
WILBERFORCE
INITIATIVE SPEAK FREEDOM

405 North Washington Street
Suite 300
Falls Church, Virginia 22046
www.21wilberforce.org
info@21wilberforce.org
571 297 3177

The Yazidis

the area, including the Peshmerga, the Sinjar Protection Units, mostly made up of Yazidis, the People's Protection Units (YPG), the Kurdistan Workers Party (PKK), as well as the Iraqi army and the Hashd al-Shaabi, or Popular Mobilization Forces.

Moving forward, like the Christians, the Yazidi's biggest concern is protection. In addition, survivors and Baba Chawish, the Yazidi spiritual leader, all indicated that in order for them to regain confidence in any security plan it must include international oversight. Without a guarantee of security and protection, the majority of Yazidis will not return to their villages.

Moreover, while the largest percentage of Yazidis are currently living in Internally Displaced People (IDP) camps, about 2,800 families have returned to Sinjar Mountain. Those living on the top of the mountain are in dire need of aid. However, due to the instability of Sinjar City, created by the tension between militia groups, those who could provide aid are often unable or unwilling. In addition, many NGOs are concerned that the next offensive against ISIS taking place in Tal Afar, just twenty minutes east of Sinjar, could send a stream of fleeing extremist fighters east through Sinjar City seeking refuge in Syria. This makes any investment in the area at this time very risky.

Complicating issues further, there have been a number of reports from local NGOs that suicide is an increasing threat to the lives of many Yazidi women and young girls affected by ISIS. Many of these women are unable to obtain proper psycho-social care due in part to a lack of available programming, but primarily as a result of a deeply entrenched honor culture that views any form of sexual uncleanliness as shameful and psychological treatment as taboo. Even though Yazidi leaders have made an effort to ensure that girls taken by ISIS are able to return to their families safely, families and communities are still ashamed by the situation. Most of the girls fear that no man will ever take them in marriage, denying them the opportunity for financial stability and physical protection. The international community needs to develop counseling programs to assist women and girls suffering from the memory of their traumatic experiences.

Yazidi girls

Bombed cars and clothes left behind by Yezidis who fled to the mountain

Policy Recommendations

IV. Policy Recommendations

1) Encourage the Senate to pass HR 390, The Iraq and Syria Genocide Accountability Act.

This bi-partisan bill, co-sponsored by Congressman Chris Smith (R- NJ) and Anna Eshoo (D- CA) authorizes and directs the State Department and USAID to use already-appropriated funds to provide humanitarian aid to minority faith and ethnic communities that have been affected by war crimes and genocide and are in desperate need of assistance. It also authorizes and directs the State Department and USAID to support criminal investigations on-the-ground in Iraq to hold members of ISIS and perpetrators of war crimes accountable. In turn, this strengthens U.S. efforts to counter terrorism and violent extremism; and it directs the Secretary of State to encourage foreign countries to add identifying information about suspected perpetrators of such crimes to their databases and security screenings.

2) Fresh Eyes on the Target

In 2005 I travelled to Iraq and what I found was a failing US policy. Following that trip I encouraged the administration to create the Iraq Study Group, also known as the Baker-Hamilton Commission, named after former Secretary of State James Baker and former Congressman Lee Hamilton of Indiana. The purpose of the bi-partisan commission was to evaluate US engagement in Iraq and propose an updated policy. I believed that "fresh eyes" on the target were needed.

Today, the United States is once again in need of "fresh eyes" in Iraq, not only for the victims of genocide, war crimes, and crimes against humanity, but also because of our critical national security interests in the region. Failure to act in the upcoming months may result in chaos and violence in Iraq once again. The lines are drawn. The militias stand ready at the berms and check points. The United States has a vested interest in

405 North Washington Street
Suite 300
Falls Church, Virginia 22046
www.21wilberforce.org
info@21wilberforce.org
571 297 3177

Policy Recommendations

promoting peace and stability in a region where over 4,000 Americans gave their lives and $2 trillion of taxpayer money was spent in the past fifteen years. I believe that we have a small window to act and if we don't, we will have squandered a unique political moment.

A high-level group of individuals with expertise in the region should be brought together to do an assessment of the current situation and make recommendations for policy going forward. People like Gen. David Petraeus and former Ambassador Ryan Crocker could head such an assessment group.

After this assessment, perhaps new top leadership should be brought together to carry out proposed policies. During my time in Congress, I visited conflict zones around the world, like Iraq. I have come to the conclusion that personnel is policy and therefore the Trump Administration should consider a new team leader to implement post-ISIS policies in Iraq, including an "Office of the Special Coordinator for Post-ISIS Iraq." This office would be responsible for coordinating NGO rebuilding projects in the region, overseeing stability operations and peace-keeping missions.

3) International Coalition to Secure the Nineveh Plains

During my visit, every Christian and Yazidi leader cited insecurity as their people's main impediment to returning home after ISIS. Protection and security are essential. While this must ultimately be determined by the Department of Defense and the State Department, many on the ground suggested a U.S. training base, or a joint-training base, in the region. Those we spoke with have great confidence in the American military and desire to have their local police and security forces trained by the US.

4) The US should utilize contractors who are able to leave the secured compound in order to build relationships, gather information and observe daily life in the region.

I understand that embassy and consular employees have security

21ST CENTURY
WILBERFORCE
INITIATIVE · SPEAK · FREEDOM

405 North Washington Street
Suite 300
Falls Church, Virginia 22046
www.21wilberforce.org
info@21wilberforce.org
571 297 3177

Note: The previous material submitted for the record is not reprinted here in its entirety but may be accessed in full on the Internet at the following address: http://docs.house.gov/Committee/Calendar/ByEvent.aspx?EventID=106459

www.yazda.org   Yazda   @YazdaOrg   info@yazda.org

Yazda Global Organization

USA: P.O.Box. 771448, Huston, TX 77215
Germany: Augsburger Str. 364, 70327 Stuttgart.
United Kingdom: 14-18 City Road, Cardiff, CF24 3DL
Sweden: Ljungdalavägen 4, 28 139 Hässleholm.
Iraq-KRI: 0, Malta- Sozdar Road, Behind Aland Motel Dohuk

Yazda
Global Yazidi Organization

Registration No: **USA**: 802053471/ **Germany**: HRB 7695083/ **UK**: 10484891/ **Sweden**: 802503-2767/ **Iraq**: 3652 CODE 2418-F

To/ Committee On Foreign Affairs
Subcommittee on Africa, Global Health, Global Human Rights, and International Organizations
U.S. House Of Representatives
Washington, DC 20515-6128
Date: Tuesday, October 3.
Time: 2:00pm
Hearing Subject: Iraq and Syria Genocide Emergency Relief and Accountability
Witness: Written Testimony By **Yazda**, A Global Yazidi Organization.

Introduction

After three years of ongoing genocide at the hands of the so-called Islamic State, or IS, the Yazidi community in Iraq and Syria continues to face an uncertain future. Some 3,000 Yazidi women and children remain in IS captivity. Hundreds of thousands of Yazidis languish in camps across Kurdistan Region of Iraq (KRI), displaced from their homeland in the Sinjar region of Northern Iraq. Those beginning to return to Sinjar find their villages and towns totally destroyed, and have no or very little support to begin the rebuilding process. Humanitarian conditions are appalling, with limited access to basic necessities such as clean water and medical supplies.

Further complicating this situation is a range of geopolitical issues, disputes between the Central Government of Iraq (CGI) and the Kurdish Regional Government of Iraq (KRG) on one side, and between political groups and militias, including, the Kurdistan Democratic Party (PDK), a group of Syrian and Turkish Kurdish fighters affiliated to the Kurdistan Workers' Party (PKK), and the Popular Mobilization Units (PMU). These competing groups and militias are vying for power in the area. Yazidis are given no say in policies that affect them, and are systematically excluded from positions of power. Finally, entrenched prejudice against the Yazidis shows no signs of abating even as IS is being defeated. Yazidis continue to be persecuted and discriminated against across all spheres of life, both in Iraq and in the KRI.

Yazda Organization

Yazda is a global Yazidi organization established in August 2014 by Yazidi students and professionals in the USA and Europe, with the aim of supporting the Yazidi community following the genocidal campaign against Yazidis by IS. Yazda was created to respond to the various needs of the displaced and traumatized Yazidi community. In addition to implementing multiple humanitarian projects, Yazda engages in public advocacy on behalf of the Yazidi people to ensure they have a voice on major political and social issues. Yazda is active in most areas inhabited by Yazidis in Iraq and in other countries where Yazidis are based. It is registered as a non-profit in the USA, KRI, Iraq, the UK, Germany, Sweden and it is in the process of registration in Australia and Canada.

The Genocide

In the early hours of 3 August 2014, IS launched a coordinated attack across the Sinjar region besieging the Yazidi population from all four sides. In accordance with IS's openly stated intention to annihilate Yazidis as a group, approximately 10,000 Yazidis were killed or abducted in the following days.[1] The perpetrators systematically divided Yazidis into different groups with particular crimes reserved for each:

* Young women and girls, some as young as 9 years of age, were forcibly converted and transferred to and between various holding sites in Iraq and Syria to be used as *sabaya* (sex slaves) or forced wives by IS fighters, a practice that was officially endorsed and regulated by IS leadership;

* Yazidi boys who had not yet reached puberty were considered to have malleable identities. They were therefore separated from their mothers, brainwashed, radicalized, and trained as child soldiers; and

* Older boys and men who refused to convert to Islam, or in some cases even those who agreed to convert under pressure, as well as some of the older women, were summarily executed by shooting or having their throats cut, their bodies often left onsite or dumped in mass graves. Those who were forced to convert to Islam and spared were relocated by IS to abandoned villages and exploited as forced laborers.

IS's attack also caused at least 250,000 Yazidis to flee to Mount Sinjar, where they were surrounded by IS for days in high temperatures and prevented from access to food, water or medical care in a deliberate attempt by IS to cause large numbers of deaths. Hundreds of Yazidis perished before a coordinated rescue operation, supported by an international coalition led by the United States, led to the opening of a safe passage to Syria.

In addition, IS destroyed Yazidi religious sites in the territories it occupied.[2] Yazidi homes and properties were destroyed or looted, severely hampering the prospects of surviving Yazidis returning to their homeland swiftly after liberation.

There is compelling evidence that a genocide took place against the Yazidis. The US House of Representatives was among the first to acknowledge that IS was committing war crimes, crimes against humanity and genocide against Yazidis, Christians and other ethno-religious minority groups.[3] Several other bodies have also recognized the crimes committed against Yazidis as genocide, including The Iraqi Council of Ministers, the European Parliament, the Council of Europe, the UK House of Commons, French Parliament, the US State Department and Congress, the Scottish Parliament and Canada's House of Commons.[4] Further, the United Nations Independent International Commission of Inquiry on the Syrian Arab Republic ('Inquiry on Syria') found in June 2016 that IS's actions against the Yazidis amounted to multiple war crimes, crimes against humanity and genocide.[5] In September 2017, after three years of advocacy by the Yazidi community, and with the strong support of the US, the UN Security Council passed UK-sponsored Resolution 2379 (2017),[6] to establish an Investigative Team to hold IS accountable by collecting, preserving, and storing evidence of acts that may amount to war crimes, crimes against humanity and genocide committed by IS in Iraq. This is an important step towards achieving justice and

---

[1] V. Cetorelli, I. Sasson, N. Shabila and G. Burnham, 'Mortality and kidnapping estimates for the Yazidi population in the area of Mount Sinjar, Iraq, in August 2014: A retrospective household survey', 9 May 2017, available at: http://journals.plos.org/plosmedicine/article?id=10.1371/journal.pmed.1002297.

[2] I. Al-Marashi, 'The impact of the Islamic State of Iraq and Syria's campaign on Yezidi religious structures and pilgrimage practices', in Pilgrimage and tourism to holy cities: ideological and management perspectives, by M. Leppakari and K.Griffin (Cabi, 2017).

[3] International Recognition of the Yazidi Genocide, USA, UK, Canada, UN, France, Scotland, Iraq, EU parliament, other states and entities have recognized that ISIS is committing genocide against the Yazidis https://www.yazda.org/the-recognition/.

[4] International Recognition of the Yazidi Genocide, USA, UK, Canada, UN, France, Scotland, Iraq, EU parliament, other states and entities have recognized that ISIS is committing genocide against the Yazidis https://www.yazda.org/the-recognition/ .

[5] Independent International Commission of Inquiry on the Syrian Arab Republic, 'They came to destroy': IS Crimes against the Yazidi, U.N. Doc. A/HRC/32/CRP.2 (Jun. 15, 2016), pp. 20-32.

[6] Security Council Requests Creation of Independent Team to Help in Holding ISIL (Da'esh) Accountable for Its Actions in Iraq, 21 SEPTEMBER 2017. http://www.un.org/press/en/2017/sc12998.doc.htm

accountability. Member states are encouraged to contribute funds in support of the implementation of the resolution, including voluntarily contributing to a trust fund that is to be established by the Secretary-General to implement the resolution. They are further encouraged to contribute equipment and services to the Investigative Team, including the offer of expert personnel; to cooperate with the Investigative Team, once established, including through mutual arrangements on legal assistance, and by providing it with any relevant information; and to provide appropriate legal assistance and capacity building to the Government of Iraq to strengthen its courts and judicial system.

The Current Situation

Yazidis still in IS captivity

It is estimated that approximately 7,000 Yazidis were captured by IS as they attacked Sinjar in August 2014.[7] The latest figures from the Directorate of Yazidi Affairs in the KRG (as of June 2017) shows that 3,048 people have been able to return to freedom from IS captivity over the last three years.[8]

However, many have died in captivity due to poor conditions and frequent violence, or while being used by IS as human shields; some have been killed during Allied airstrikes to liberate IS-controlled areas such as Mosul and Tal Afar.[9]

Further, neither the Iraqi authorities nor the international community have taken meaningful action to assist or rescue the over 3,000 women and children still in captivity.[10] In many cases, their location was known at some point, as was the identity of their captors, and some of the captives remained in telephone contact with their families in camps for IDPs in the KRI. Nevertheless, while there have been reports of raids by Peshmerga and US forces to free foreign and Iraqi citizens,[11] Yazda is not aware of such raids having been organized to rescue the Yazidis kept in slavery by IS.

Survivors of captivity

The long-term physical and psychological health issues facing Yazidi survivors are significant, and the need for specialized, fully-funded medical assistance and trauma counseling is high. There is a risk of suicide among Yazidi women and girls who have escaped IS captivity, along with other long-term effects of sexual and gender based violence. Yazidi boys recruited by IS to undergo forced conversion and military training require ongoing psychological support to address the impact such abuse has caused.   Humanitarian aid workers have identified a serious lack of ongoing and intensive mental health and psychosocial support services in camps and shelters, while the need only increases as towns are liberated and severely traumatized captives return to freedom. Most survivors require long term treatment outside Iraq for critical conditions that cannot be treated effectively in Iraq, Yazda acknowledges the importance of resettlement programs by Germany, Canada and Australia, Yazda hope that USA will join these countries to welcome survivors and their families.

---

[7] The precise number of Yazidis taken captive is unknown, so estimates have varied from 7,000 (J Stern & JM Berger, *IS: The State of Terror* (Harper Collins, 2015) 216) and 6,800 (V. Cetorelli, I. Sasson, N. Shabila and G. Burnham, 'Mortality and kidnapping estimates for the Yazidi population in the area of Mount Sinjar, Iraq, in August 2014: A retrospective household survey', 9 May 2017, available at: http://journals.plos.org/plosmedicine/article?id=10.1371/journal.pmed.1002297).

[8] Office of the High Commissioner for Human Rights, *Accountability and reconciliation key to heal Iraq's ISIL wounds – Zeid*, 11 July 2017, available at: http://www.ohchr.org/EN/NewsEvents/Pages/DisplayNews.aspx?NewsID=21860&LangID=E.

[9] OHCHR, *Mosul: ISIL use of 'human shields' underscores need to protect civilians – Zeid*, 21 October 2016, available at: http://www.ohchr.org/EN/NewsEvents/Pages/DisplayNews.aspx?NewsID=20729.

[10] The UN estimated in July 2017 that 3,396 Yazidis remained in ISIS captivity, see OHCHR, Accountability and reconciliation key to heal Iraq's ISIL wounds, July 2017, available at www.ohchr.org/EN/NewsEvents/Pages/DisplayNews.aspx?NewsID=21860&LangID=E .

[11] Reuters, 'Kurdish special forces rescue Swedish girl from Islamic State', 23 February 2016, available at: http://www.reuters.com/article/us-mideast-crisis-islamicstate-hostage-idUSKCN0VW18J, The Guardian, Iraq rescue: video shows US prison raid freeing 70 hostages from IS, 24 October 2015, available at https://www.theguardian.com/world/2015/oct/25/video-released-us-kurdish-rescue-operation-iraq-isis-hawija

Displacement

IS's advance over Northern Iraq has caused unprecedented levels of forced displacement among the communities, including the Yazidi population. According to the UN Inquiry on Syria, in the aftermath of the attack "no free Yazidis remained in the Sinjar region ... [t]he 400,000-strong community had all been displaced, captured, or killed".[12] Today, there are an estimated 340,000 Yazidis living in IDP camps in the KRI, around 85% of Yazidi the entire Yazidi community in Iraq, while a further 90,000 have fled from Iraq since 2014.[13] Countries including Germany, Canada, Australia, France, the Netherlands and Portugal have taken in substantial numbers of Yazidi refugees. Currently, there are also around 1,800 Iraqi-Yazidis in Turkey, 1,500 in Syria and 1,000 in Greece. The number of Syrian-Yazidis who sought refuge in Jordan, Lebanon, and Turkey is unknown.

As a result of systematic persecution under successive governments in Syria, Turkey and Iraq and because of the increasing extremist ideology in these areas the Yazidis have been actively targeted and remove from the Middle East. In Iraq, the Yazidi population decreased from 750.000 in 2005 to 550.000 in 2014 and this number further decreased to 90.000 in 2017.[14] In Syria, an estimated 150,000 Yazidis inhabited 110 villages and towns in the Aleppo and Hasakah regions until the unrest erupted in 2011, but this number has decreased to less than 10.000 by 2017. In Turkey there are around 300 Yazidis left today from the total population of over 80.000 in 1970.[15]

Those Yazidis living in IDP camps live in appalling conditions, with inadequate humanitarian support. Among other concerns, Yazidis in IDP camps in the KRI frequently mention unreliable electricity (few hours a day), the poor state of tents which have not been replaced for three years and are not warm enough for next winter, the air quality due to the burning of garbage in and nearby the camps, the deteriorating sanitation and damaged sewage system which has led to outbreaks of disease, a lack of access to clean drinking water; and insufficient medical care.

Returning IDPs

Survivors of the genocide, including those who were able to flee before being captured, yearn have not been able to return to their homeland as the lack assurances of security, peace and stability. Rates of return have increased since July 2017 to about 60 to 120 families per day. However, fewer than 52,000 Yazidis have returned to Sinjar, and fewer than 10,000 in Bashiqa and Bahzani in total. There are a number of factors preventing Yazidis from returning to their homes.

In particular, entire villages and towns were destroyed by IS and there remains a shortage of inhabitable homes and suitable infrastructure. Many buildings are still covered with landmines and other explosives. According to the Mayor of Sinjar, Mahama Khalil, about 80-85% of Sinjar District has been destroyed by IS and rebuilding the district will require significant investment.[16]

Exacerbating the security situation is the in-fighting between various factions and armed groups, creating fear among the Yazidi population and impeding the rebuilding process by restricting the movement of goods and denying permission to liberated areas. Since the liberation of some Yazidi areas in 2015, no new service projects have been initiated because of this economic blockade.[17] Further, the lack of essential services such as the provision of clean drinking water, electricity and

[12] Independent International Commission of Inquiry on the Syrian Arab Republic, "They came to destroy": IS Crimes against the Yazidi, U.N. Doc. A/HRC/32/CRP.2 (Jun. 15, 2016), p. 33

[13] Iraqi News, July 13, 2017, available at http://www.iraqinews.com/iraq-war/90000-yazidis-fled-iraq-since-emergence-kurdishofficial/

[14] Refworld, July 10, 2014, available at http://www.refworld.org/docid/54bf62684.html; Yazidi Council in Syria, March 10, 2012, available at http:// ezidenrat.de/?page_id=136

[15] 115684-جولة-الباحث-في-قرى-ايزيدية؟Bahzani net July 2, 2016, available at http://www.bahzani.net/services/forum/showthread.php [51] This figure does not include Yazidis who have been displaced to Turkey following IS's attack on Sinjar and live in makeshift تركيا; refugee camps.

[16] NRT, available at http://www.nrttv.com/AR/Detail.aspx?Jimare=22196; Alsumaria TV, April 28, 2016, available at http:// www.alsumaria.tv/mobile/news/166898/البر ان-يصوت-على-اعتبار-سنجار-مدينة-منك/ar .

[17] HRW, December 4, 2016, available at https://www.hrw.org/news/2016/12/04/iraq-krg-restrictions-harm-yazidi-recovery

fuel, and access to basic medical services makes the living conditions in these regions extremely hard.

Denial of rights and ongoing discrimination and disempowerment

The Yazidis are among the world's most marginalized communities suffering continuing persecution in Iraq including in the KRI, Turkey and Syria. Historically, Yazidis have been prohibited from building religious centers or practicing their faith freely in Syria and Turkey and to some extend in Iraq, despite Iraq being home to Yazidism's holiest sites; they are still discriminated against systemically. They are not allowed to hold positions of authority over Muslims (such as judges) – with only few exceptions in the KRI. Yazidi-made food products are not considered Halal and are therefore not eaten by almost all Muslims. Efforts are continually made to strip the Yazidi minority of their true identity, land, and to exclude them from any political and social involvement. This disempowerment continues today in a range of ways.

<u>Education</u>

Education is crucial for vulnerable minorities such as the Yazidis so as to be equipped with skills and knowledge that will ultimately empower individuals and their community. For decades, however, the Yazidis and other Iraqi minorities encountered institutional discrimination in the education sector, and this continues to be the case both in Iraq and within the KRI today. Yazidi areas were deliberately excluded from the KRG and Iraqi education plan that resulted in the construction of thousands of schools, institutes and universities across the country since 2003. In addition, disputes over Yazidi areas between the KRG and CGI meant that although the Arabic curriculum is necessary to be eligible for Iraqi universities, the KRG offered only the Kurdish curriculum in its schools. The Yazidi student continue to suffer the implications of the two systems, which results in many students not being able to complete their educational programs. Further, many schools in Sinjar lacked and continue to lack staff.

IS's occupation of Sinjar exacerbated existing problems. Most of the schools in Yazidi villages were destroyed and very few in the northern side of the district were re-opened. Thousands of Yazidis were forced to leave school and have now been out of the education system for over three years. Although international NGOs such as UNICEF provide education programs in some IDP camps in the KRI, these are insufficient to meet the needs of thousands of Yazidi children. There remain issues with lack of staff, security, unsafe buildings, and basic services such as electricity and drinking water. Access to schooling by Yazidi children has been worsened by the presence of armed forces in the area and difficulties in returning to Sinjar.

Security issues along with the defacto control of various groups on administration impedes re-establishing schools in the liberated areas.

Financial and employment challenges

As a result of the genocide perpetrated by IS, Yazidis have lost almost everything they once owned. The vast majority fled their homes with only a few clothes and personal belongings, leaving behind properties and official documents. IS looted Yazidi possessions and destroyed most of their houses, schools, institutions and religious shrines in the Sinjar and Nineveh Plain regions. As well as having no remaining assets, Yazidi IDPs and refugees face unemployment and poverty. The unemployment rate in Yazidi areas in Iraq and KRI is over 70%, much higher than in any other region, as Yazidis continue to suffer employment discrimination on the basis of their religion and due to lack of jobs generally.[18]

---

[18] Waad Matto, the head of Yazidi Progress Party in an open message to Masoud Barzani, the Kurdistan 46 President, June 11, 2011, available at http://spyav.alafdal.net/t40-topic

Reducing discrimination against Yazidis via education programs and legislative changes would assist Yazidis to access the job market. Options for governments to consider include a monthly financial assistance program for those with special needs (orphans, those with medical conditions, etc), and a micro-financing scheme that could provide small grants or loans to assist Yazidi families in setting up small businesses.

Discriminatory laws and property ownership

Civil laws in Iraq and the KRI are sometimes openly discriminatory against the Yazidis. For example, under Article 26 of the Iraqi National Identity Card, when a non-Muslim parent converts to Islam, their children will be registered as Muslim, regardless of the will of the second parent or the children themselves. On the other hand, conversion from Islam to any other religion is forbidden. No personal status law exists to decide on cases related to the rights of the Yazidi such as marriage, divorcement, or ownership of property. Indeed, Yazidi rights to ownership are not recognized in Iraqi law. Thus, most of the properties belonging to Yazidis in Sinjar are not legally owned by them.[19] In addition, hatred toward Yazidis is frequently promoted in the mosques and by Muslim Preachers while there is no enforcement of laws (and there is no law that we are aware of) that criminalize hate speeches against the Yazidis or other minorities.

Civil and political rights

Yazidis of the Sinjar and Shehkan districts are *de facto* part of the KRI region, but do not have the right to vote in KRI elections on the basis that the Yazidi areas are not a formally recognized part of the KRI. In a clear discriminatory and unjust treatment by the KRI, the Yazidis were included in the September 2017 Kurdish Independence Referendum, however, they will be excluded from the KRI elections set for November 2017. Yazidis have, until recently, not been permitted to create their own political parties in Iraq, and even now the views of Yazidi organizations and leaders are not taken into account when policy decisions are made by major political parties, governments and parliaments in either Iraq or the KRI.[20]

Posts for local governments, mayors and municipalities in the Yazidi areas are not elected, but are rather appointed by political parties, mainly by the PDK. This underrepresentation or outright exclusion of Yazidis from political processes serves to entrench Yazidi disempowerment and prevent Yazidi voices from being heard in relation to matters that affect the community. Yazidis are underrepresented in all key institutions in both Iraq and the KRI, as they have little opportunity to make changes to government policy or programs. The CGI and KRG, both drawn from multiple political factions, have no Yazidi participation at the ministerial level; the Iraqi and KRI Parliaments have only two Yazidi MPs in Baghdad (out of 328 MPs) and only one Yazidi MP in Erbil (out of 111 MPs). Government institutions have no or limited representation by Yazidis,[21] and almost no access to important military positions within the Iraqi military and Kurdish Peshmerga.

The suppression of certain political opinions and the refusal to accept Yazidi identity remain serious issues. Yazidis in the KRI are discriminated against when they refuse to self-identify as Kurdish; for example, gaining a residency card or driver's license is impossible unless a Yazidi registers as ethnically Kurdish. Only those Yazidis who consider themselves Kurdish have been able to obtain senior positions in the KRI leadership.[22]

---

[19] Bahzani net, December 10, 2013, available at http://www.bahzani.nat/services/forum/showthread.php? في-ملة-كاصية-- 70475 ; Almadapress, November 11, 2015, available at http://www.almadapress.com/ar/ ;سنجار-من-دون-سندات-تمليك-نادور-السكنية
NewsDetails.aspx?NewsID= 60507 منظمتان دوليتان تكشفان عن مشروع لإعمار سنجار ودخيل تطالب بتمليك منازل الايزيديين

[20] USCRIF.GOV, May 7, 2017, available at http://www.uscirf.gov/sites/default/files/KurdistanReport_short_FINAL_lowres.pdf,

[21] Alsumaria TV, January 12, 2017, available at http://www.alsumaria.tv/news/ /لحق-العليا-المفوضية-اعضاء-اسماء-تنشر-نيوز-السومرية /210419
ar

[22] USCRIF.GOV, July 28, 2014, available at https://www.state.gov/j/drl/rls/irf/2013/nea/222291.htm.

Geopolitical and military complications in the Yazidi homeland

Sinjar is an important geopolitical territory. Located within Iraq, it borders Syria and Turkey. It serves as a decisive buffer zone between the Syrian Kurdish territory, Rojava, and the KRI. Control and sovereignty over Sinjar territory is disputed between the CGI, the local Nineveh government, and the KRG. Key international, regional and local parties have sought to influence the situation in the region with differing visions and agendas, into which the Yazidi population is given no say, and which has the overall effect of keeping Yazidis powerless in determining their own future. Control over the territories that are occupied, at least in part, by the Yazidi population has been, and continues to be, subject to constant challenge.[23] As well as concerns about the instability caused by disputes of control of the area, there is also a concern about the informal militarization of Yazidi communities in Sinjar and the Nineveh Plain by the PMU, Iraqi Kurdish parties and the PKK, outside the framework of the state's law and military apparatus. In some cases, Yazda has become aware of the recruitment of Yazidi children, which constitutes a grave violation of international and national laws. The 25 September Kurdish Independence Referendum added further dimensions to the already complex political situation for Yazidis.

The November's Referendum is expected to further complicate the situation in Sinjar and Nineveh Plain, the PMU and/or the Iraqi might use the force to control these areas as they see Kurdish de facto rule is illegitimate.

Recommendations for the US Congress

<u>Justice and accountability</u>

1. Investigate and prosecute the perpetrators of IS's crimes against the Yazidis where possible in US courts, including by using all available means of mutual legal assistance such as the extradition to the US of its nationals suspected of having committed, as a member of IS, international crimes, including war crimes, crimes against humanity and genocide, against the Yazidis, and to provide all available means of legal assistance and support to other national, international and/or hybrid investigations and prosecutions of crimes committed by IS against the Yazidis where these are consistent with international due process standards.

2. Fully cooperate with, and support, the Investigative Team to be established pursuant to United Nations Security Council Resolution 2379 (2017) in its collection, preservation and storage of evidence of acts that may amount to war crimes, crimes against humanity and genocide committed by ISIS in Iraq. Specifically, Resolution 2379 calls on member states to:

<u>Security and protection of Yazidis</u>

1. Coordinate intelligence and technical and/or military support to rescue the over 3,000 Yazidis who remain in captivity.

2. Continue efforts to defeat IS militarily and reduce its influence ideologically via deradicalization programs.

3. Support the establishment of a security zone / protected area in Sinjar and Nineveh Plain for Yazidis, Christian and other minorities, under the supervision of the United Nations and in cooperation with minorities living in these areas, for a transitional period of three to five years.

4. Support an international mediation process to negotiate an ultimate solution for the disputed areas between the KRI and CGI, in consultation with the groups who live in these regions, to apply after the transitional period.

---

[23] http://www.al-monitor.com/pulse/originals/2017/05/iraq-kurdistan-peshmerga-pmu-sinjar.html; http://www.al-monitor.com/pulse/originals/2017/03/turkey-iraqi-kurdistan-ankara-is-getting-entangled-sinjar.html; http://www.al-monitor.com/pulse/originals/ 2017/05/ turkey-iraq-sinjar-what-is-happening-in-yazidi-land.html

5. Encourage a new and transparent election process for Municipality and District Levels in Iraq and KRI which facilitates equal participation by all groups in the area, with representatives from each community.

6. Support the protection and preservation of two major Yazidi religious sites: Lalish and Sharfaddeen temple under international regulations for the protection of heritage sites.

Resettlement of Yazidis in the USA

1. Consider the critical situation of the Yazidi population in all US immigration and refugees' admission programs.

2. Admit victims of Genocide and sexual enslavement and their families into the USA through a program similar to Germany, Canada, and Australia.

3. Expedite International Organization Migration program to resettle families of those who supported US military or institutions. Yazda can provide a list of pending cases.

Humanitarian assistance

1. Support the rebuilding of Sinjar and humanitarian needs of returning Yazidis, by establishing a fund dedicated to the rebuilding critical infrastructure in Yazidi areas, to be administered and supervised efficiently and transparently.

2. Provide assistance with the removal of landmines in liberated areas.

3. Encourage authorities in Iraq and KRI to facilitate the movement of goods and building materials, and allow access to liberated areas to allow for the reconstruction process to begin.

4. Provide support to survivors of the Yazidi Genocide, with a focus on those with particular needs such as women and girls who suffered sexual violence, boys who have survived IS captivity, and survivors with serious medical issues. Develop and support evidence-based programs for effective psychological assistance.

5. Fund medical care for Yazidis in Iraq and KRI, and provide access to overseas medical treatment for Yazidi survivors.

6. Take into account the needs of the Yazidi community in the development of humanitarian / refugee programs, and consider the Yazidi population as a priority group for resettlement, given ongoing humanitarian concerns and persecution.

7. Support the needs of Yazidis in education and health, by supporting the rebuilding of educational facilities in the Sinjar region, funding the construction of a university in Sinjar, and providing scholarships to Yazidi students to study outside of Iraq.

A detailed new report about the current situation of the Yazidis can be found via this link https://www.yazda.org/wp-content/uploads/2017/06/Yazda-Report-2017_an-Uncertain-Future-for-Yazidis_A-Report-Marking-Three-Years-of-an-Ongoing-Genocide.pdf.

For more information, please contact:
- Haider Elias, Yazda President, on helias@yazda.org
- Murad Ismael, Yazda Executive Director on murad.ismael@yazda.org
- Ahmed Khudida Burjus, Yazda Deputy Executive Director, on ahmed.kudida@yazda.org
- Abid Shamdeen, Yazda Director for Government Relations, on abidshamdeen@gmail.com

Or call us:
- USA: +1 (832) 298-9584
- Europe: +44 (749) 506-2635

Questions for the Record
Submitted by Chairman Chris Smith
"Iraq and Syria Genocide Emergency Relief and Accountability"
October 3, 2017

<u>**Legal Counsel, Director of Internationally Displaced Persons Assistance Chaldean Catholic Archdiocese of Erbil. Mr. Steve Rasche**</u>

EWTN News Nightly asked the U.S. Agency for International Development to respond to your testimony. The response, attributed to a "U.S. official" was "Any assertion that the U.S. is not providing support to vulnerable communities in Iraq is false. It is also false to claim the United State has not provided assistance that reaches Christians and other minority communities in Iraq."

What is your response to this statement?

My testimony was not that the US was not expending funds to support vulnerable communities, including Christians. My testimony was instead that any such expenditures were not effectively reaching these communities. Furthermore, I specifically addressed the issue of reporting from the UNDP and others, which purported to show that since funds were being spent that therefore benefits were necessarily being received by these vulnerable communities. These reports were grossly misleading, and in many cases factually incorrect. This is now widely acknowledged, and subsequent reporting by the UNDP, which corrects these areas, is proof of this.

Regarding the formulaic response of the un-named USAID spokesperson, despite numerous requests from members of Congress and concerned private groups, no person or entity within the US government has been able as of this date to address, with any meaningful level of detail, what actual work was performed which actually reached the vulnerable Christian communities during the time in question. Furthermore, the factual failure of US backed aid to reach these vulnerable communities was also attested to at the same hearing by former Congressman Frank Wolf, who had recently returned from a fact finding trip to the region.